McDougal Littell

Strategies *for* Test Preparation

HIGH SCHOOL

McDougal Littell

A HOUGHTON MIFFLIN COMPANY

Evanston, Illinois • Boston • Dallas

Acknowledgments

Page: 13: Excerpt from *The Analects of Confucius,* translated and annotated by Arthur Waley. Copyright © 1938 by George Allen & Unwin, copyright renewed 1966. Reprinted by permission of Scribner, a division of Simon & Schuster, Inc. and the Estate of Arthur Waley.

Page 15: Excerpt from *The Log of Christopher Columbus,* translated by Robert H. Fuson. Copyright © 1987 by Robert H. Fuson. Reprinted by permission of the author.

Page 17: Excerpt from "Russian Organised Crime," from *The Economist,* August 28, 1999. Copyright © 1999 The Economist. Reprinted by permission.

Page 18: Excerpts from "Tariff and Nullification," from *The Complete Book of U.S. Presidents* by William A. DeGregorio. Copyright © 1984, 1989, 1991, 1993 by William A. DeGregorio. Reprinted by permission of Barricade Books Inc.

Page 21: Daniel Fitzpatrick cartoon: "Next!" Swastica rolling over Poland. Reprinted with permission of the Saint Louis Post-Dispatch, 2001.

Page 22: Toles cartoon, "well, well, well, let me guess." Toles Copyright © 2001 The Buffalo News. Reprinted with permission of Universal Press Syndicate. All Rights Reserved.

Page 23: Cy Hungerford cartoon: "Time Flies, so does Harry." Copyright © Cy Hungerford/Pittsburgh Post-Gazette, 2002. All Rights Reserved. Reprinted with permission.

Page 30: "Cumulative Production of CFCs: 1958–1994" and "Voter Turnout in the United States, By Age: 1996" from *A Statistical Portrait of the United States: Social Conditions and Trends,* edited by Mark S. Littman. Copyright © 1998 Bernan Press, an imprint of Bernan Associates, a division of Kraus Organization Limited. Reprinted by permission.

Page 33: Adapted from "A working day in the life of a 10-year old girl in Nepal," from *Listening to Smaller Voices* by Victoria Johnson, Joanna Hill, and Edda Ivan-Smith. Copyright © 1995 by ActionAid Nepal. Reprinted by permission.

Page 34: "Selected Metropolitan Areas Minority Populations, 1990 (Percent)," from *Atlas of American Diversity* by Larry Hajime Shinagawa and Michael Jang. Copyright © 1998 by AltaMira Press. Reprinted by permission of AltaMira Press, a division of Sage Publications, Inc.

Page 35: "Government Expenditures, 1992 (United States)", "Government Expenditures, 1992 (Israel)" and "Government Expenditures, 1992 (India)" from *Statistical Abstracts of the World,* edited by Marlita A. Reddy. Copyright © 1992 by Gale Research Inc. Reprinted by permission of the Gale Group.

Page 53: "Causes of Death, 1993," from *Oxford Atlas of World History,* edited by Patrick K. O'Brien. Copyright © 1999 by Oxford University Press. All rights reserved. Reprinted by permission of Oxford University Press.

Page 54: Excerpt from "TV Comment on Joseph McCarthy, 1954" by Edward R. Murrow, from *In Search of Light: The Broadcasts of Edward R. Murrow, 1938–1961,* edited by Edward Bliss, Jr. Copyright © 1967 by the Estate of Edward R. Murrow. Reprinted by permission of Random House, Inc.

Page 57: Mongol Warrior. Copyright © Victoria and Albert Museuam, London/Art Resource, New York.

Page 59: Patricia Zelewski, Liverpool High School, Liverpool, New York.

Page 61: Jacob Riis photo of immigrants sleeping in tenement. The Granger Collection, New York.

Page 62: *The Great Chicago Fire, 1871.* The Granger Collection, New York.

Page 62: *The San Francisco Earthquake, 1906.* Copyright © Bettmann/Corbis.

Page 64: Excerpt from "Andrew Smith Hallidie" by Edgar Myron Kahn, Museum of the City of San Francisco web site (http://www.sfmuseum.org). Reprinted by permission of the Museum of the City of San Francisco.

Page 66: *Fifth Avenue at Madison Square,* 1894–1895 by Theodore Robinson. Oil on canvas 24 1/8 x 19 1/4 in. (61.3 x 48.9 cm). Gift of Ferdinand Howald, Columbus Museum of Art.

ISBN 0-618-20284-6

Printed in the United States of America.

11 12 13 14 15 -MDO- 09 08 07 06

Table of Contents

You can prepare for tests as you would for any other assignment you are given during the school year. The materials in this booklet will boost your achievement level in history and social science.

Content Overview

Each part of this booklet gives a different type of support that can become part of your daily study habits.

Part 1: General Strategies for Taking Tests

Tips for Successful Testing This section gives strategies you can use during the school year to help you prepare for tests. It also provides tips you can use during the testing.

Vocabulary for Testing Situations In this section you'll find brief definitions of words often used on standardized tests and terms taught in social science texts.

Part 2: Test-Taking Strategies and Practice

This part of the book provides tutorials and practice in the types of items that appear on many types of social studies tests. Each tutorial offers instruction and practice in the content areas of world geography, world history, or U.S. history. Practice items usually include an "exhibit" of some sort, followed by multiple-choice, constructed-response, or extended-response questions— and you'll even have a chance to practice writing for a document-based question (DBQ). Exhibits include:

- Primary sources
- Secondary sources
- Political cartoons
- Charts
- Time lines
- Physical maps
- Thematic maps
- Pie graphs
- Line graphs and bar graphs

Part 3: SAT and ACT Practice

This part of the book provides strategies that will help you perform well on the reading sections of the SAT I and ACT. The material begins with an introduction to the SAT I and ACT reading subtests. Nine practice tests—consisting of a reading passage with questions—are drawn from U.S. history. Five practice tests are drawn from world history. These practice tests cover material that will increase your knowledge of history whether or not you practice test-taking skills with them.

Part 1: General Strategies for Taking Tests

Tips for Successful Testing

There are many ways you can prepare for tests. These practices can reinforce your daily learning in class, both in social studies and in other content areas. Knowledge of test-taking techniques doesn't replace knowledge of content, but it can help you learn how to use the test to demonstrate what you really know. You shouldn't lose points simply because you don't know how to take a standardized test. The following tips give you some general suggestions on how to approach a test; you'll find more detailed instruction and practice in Part 2: Test-Taking Strategies and Practice.

During the School Year

1. **Master the content of your social studies courses.** The best way to study for tests is to study, understand, and review the content of your social studies class, whether you're taking history, geography, government, or economics. Read your daily assignments carefully, and review the text and your classroom notes on a weekly basis. If you do these, you will do well on tests.

2. **Practice with testing vocabulary.** Review the lists that begin on page 5. Your teacher may build some of these words into informal and formal assessments. For words that can be used in a variety of ways, make sure you understand the particular meaning the words have in the context of testing. Try to use history/social science vocabulary during class and in homework assignments.

3. **Practice taking tests.** Use copies of past tests to practice taking a test with time limits. Learning how to effectively use your time is an important test-taking skill.

4. **Practice reading and interpreting visual representations of information.** Your textbook has many examples of charts, graphs, maps, political cartoons, and graphic organizers. Become familiar with how these visuals work, and the ways in which they present information.

5. **Interact with your own textbook.** Practice responding to assessment questions in your textbook, both orally and in writing. Try summarizing or paraphrasing longer passages.

6. **Build your stamina for long testing sessions.**
   a. Brainstorm appropriate ways to take short breaks during a timed session. You can try deep breathing, stretching, and so on.
   b. Think of strategies you've used before when you've had to concentrate for a long interval, and see how they might be applied to the testing situation.

7. **Learn to analyze the test questions.** Often, test questions seem awkward because they are written using language and/or formats that are unfamiliar or uncommon.
   a. Try paraphrasing the question in order to better understand it.
   b. Identify the type of information asked for in each question.

8. **Learn to skim materials.** Practice running your eyes quickly over texts, looking at headings, graphic features, and highlighted words. Learn to pick key words and phrases out of materials.

9. **Discuss test experiences immediately afterward.** After classroom tests and quizzes throughout the year, talk with your teacher and classmates about the experience. What strategies did you and your classmates use to come up with your answers? Were your choices effective?

Several Weeks Before the Test

As the date for a test approaches, begin to prepare specifically for the types of items you might find in the test. Here are general tips for item types that you'll have a chance to practice answering later in this book.

1. **Multiple-Choice Questions** Remember, test writers may set traps. In a well-constructed item, each wrong answer represents a mistake that might be made by a test taker who is careless or doesn't know the material. Use the following strategies with a multiple-choice items.

    a. Read and consider the question (this part is called the *stem*) carefully *before* reading the alternative answers.

    b. Pay close attention to key words in the question. For instance, look for the word *not,* as in "Which of the following was *not* a cause of the Civil War?"

    c. Consider all the alternatives before making a choice.

    d. Eliminate any answers that you know are wrong. Often you will be able to eliminate alternatives that are weaker than the others, leaving a choice between the strongest two.

       • Look for two choices that appear to boil down to the same idea. Both must be wrong.

       • Read the stem and each answer as a sentence. Does this sentence make grammatical and logical sense? Eliminate alternatives that do not "read in" logically.

       • When an answer is over qualified, it may be incorrect. Look for words like *always, never, none, all,* and *only* as a tip-off.

    e. When in doubt about an answer, try these ideas to find the correct answer:

       • If one choice is much longer and more detailed than the others, it is often the correct answer.

       • If a word in a choice also appears in the question, it should be strongly considered as the correct choice.

       • If two choices are direct opposites, one of them likely is the correct answer.

       • If one choice includes one or more of the other choices, it is often the correct answer.

       • If *some* or *often* is used in a choice, it should be strongly considered as the correct answer.

       • If *all of the above* is a choice, determine whether at least two of the other choices seem appropriate before selecting it.

       • If one response is more precise or technical, it is more likely to be correct than a general response.

2. **Constructed-Response Items** Constructed-response items can have many forms. You may have to read a paragraph, graph, chart, map, or graphic organizer, to extract information, and to make an inference or draw a conclusion. You might have to create a map, graph, or graphic organizer yourself. Use these strategies for approaching a constructed-response item.

    a. Read the directions and analyze the steps required. Read through the entire question or questions before answering.

    b. Look for key words in the prompt and plan your answer accordingly. Does the question ask you to identify a cause-and-effect relationship or to compare and contrast? Are you looking for a sequence or making a generalization?

    c. Plan your answer. If you are writing more than a few words, jot down notes and supporting details you may wish to use in your response.

    d. Target your answer. When writing your response, don't just include everything you can think of, hoping that some part of it will be correct.

    e. Support your statements with examples and details.

3. **Extended-Response Items** Extended-response questions, like constructed-response questions, usually focus on a document of some kind. However, they are more complex and require more time to complete than short-answer constructed-response questions. Use the following strategies with extended-response items.

    a. Carefully read the question and determine what it asks you to do.

    b. Analyze the document and make notes on material that may apply to the question.

    c. If the question requires an essay or other piece of writing, jot down ideas in outline form. Use the outline to write your answer.

During Test Administration

Keep the following points in mind while taking a standardized test.

1. **Read the directions.** There may be slight differences among similar directions that could make a significant difference.

2. **Take a second look.** Recheck your answers to make sure you haven't made a mistake in your markings.

3. **Pay special attention when using a separate answer sheet.** It is easy to drop down one line and accidentally throw off the answers. Use any or all of the following techniques.

    a. Use a guide, such as a ruler, on the answer sheet to keep from marking answers on the wrong line.

    b. Check every five answers or so to make sure that the appropriate line is filled for each answer.

    c. Each time you turn a page, make sure the question and answer lines match.

    d. Fill in blanks carefully and neatly and beware of stray pencil marks.

    e. Fold the test booklet so that only one page is showing at a time.

4. **As a last resort, make an educated guess.** When there is no penalty for guessing on a multiple-choice item, it's better to guess at an answer than to leave it blank. Try to eliminate one or two choices first.

5. **Rely on facts or data in the question**—not on personal preferences—when answering questions. Pay close attention to information provided in graphs, charts, or quotations when coming up with your answer.

6. **Ration your time.** Answering all of the questions will increase your chances for a better score, so you should make sure to finish the test. Pay attention to the time, and work to maintain an appropriate pace. Calculate in advance how many questions you need to answer by the halfway mark, but remember that some question formats may take you longer than others.

Vocabulary for Testing Situations

The following vocabulary words can help you prepare for tests. The first vocabulary list contains words often used in test materials. The accompanying definitions show how each word would most likely be used in a test situation, but may not be the only definitions.

The second list consists of vocabulary words taken from social studies textbooks. They are words that might prove helpful in testing situations.

Test Vocabulary

according to as stated in

action act, step, endeavor

affect influence, change

analyze break down into parts and explain relationships

apparent clear, obvious

appropriate suitable, correct

argument reason offered in proof for or against an idea

characterize represent, symbolize, show qualities of

classified arranged into groups according to specific categories

combined joined, united

compare/contrast explore similarities and differences

condition situation, circumstances

contribute add to, assist

correspond to conform, match, fit

current at the present time

data information, facts, figures

define give the exact meaning of

depend upon be determined by

describe give key information about

determine decide

development progress, growth

draw a conclusion make a judgment based on certain ideas/facts

emphasize stress, focus on, feature

evaluate judge the value of

event something that happens in a particular time/place

example illustration, representation

except all but, everything other than

excerpt selection, portion of a text

expanding growing, increasing

explain make clear and understandable

former previous, earlier

foundation base, support for conclusion

generalization general statement based on many examples

graph visual representation of facts/figures

identify find, pick out

impact affect, influence

indicate show, point out

inference a conclusion based on deduction, an informed guess

intend plan, design

interpret give your opinion, supported with reasons and details

involve be a part of

major significant, important

minor small, insignificant

occur happen

passage part of a written work, text

point location, position, main idea

primary main, most important

principle a basic law or truth

probably most likely

provide offer, supply

refer to use as a source of information

regulate control, manage

relate show the relationship or link between things

result findings, report

select choose

sequence order, arrangement

significant important, meaningful

similar nearly alike

topic subject

valid logical, suitable

History/Social Studies Vocabulary

Civics/Government

administration a particular president's term of office

Bill of Rights first ten amendments to the U.S. Constitution

bureaucracy a system of departments and agencies that carry out the work of the government

checks and balances measures designed to prevent one branch of the government from dominating another

elector a voter

impeachment the process of accusing a public official of wrongdoing

judicial review Supreme Court's power to declare an act of Congress unconstitutional

legislation law, bill, statute

naturalization a way to give full citizenship to a person born in another country

ruling official or legal decision

suffrage the right to vote

treaty agreement between nations

Culture

civilization a form of culture characterized by cities, specialized workers, complex institutions, record keeping, and advanced technology

culture a people's unique way of life

ethnic racial, cultural

population citizens, people

society community, a social order

system organization, structure

urban relating to cities or towns

Economics

capitalism economic system based on private ownership and the investment of money for profit

communism economic and political system based on one-party government and state ownership of property and production

demand willingness and ability of consumers to spend money for goods and services

economy system for the management of resources

depression a severe economic slump

free enterprise economic system in which business can be conducted freely based on the choices of individuals

goods material things that can be bought and sold

inflation an increase in the price of goods and services and a decrease in the value of money

recession an economic slump, less severe than a depression

services work performed for others

share portion of a company's stock

supply amount of economic goods available for sale

tariff a tax on imported goods

taxes money paid to the government for its support

Geography

area region, section of land bound by common characteristics

boundary border, dividing line

canyon a narrow, deep valley with steep sides

cape a pointed piece of land extending into an ocean or lake

climate conditions, such as wind, rainfall, and temperature, that are common in a region

delta a marshy region formed by silt deposits at the mouth of a river

desert a dry area where few plants grow

desertification transformation of fertile land into desert

environment habitat, climate

flood plain flat land near the edges of rivers formed by mud and silt deposited by floods

glacier a large ice mass that moves slowly down a mountain or over land

harbor a sheltered area of water deep enough for docking ships

hemisphere half of the globe

island a body of land surrounded by water

latitude distance in degrees north or south of the earth's equator

location position

longitude distance in degrees east or west of the prime meridian at Greenwich, England

plateau a broad, flat area of land higher than the surrounding land

prairie a large, level area of grassland with few or no trees

projection a way of showing the curved surface of the earth on a flat map

region geographical area

scale ratio between a unit of length on a map and a unit of distance on the earth

steppe a wide, treeless plain

strait a narrow strip of water connecting two large bodies of water

swamp an area of land that is saturated by water

valley low land between hills or mountains

volcano an opening in the earth through which gasses and lava escape from the earth's interior

History

apartheid South African policy of complete legal and social separation of the races

aristocracy government in which the power is in the hands of a hereditary ruling class or nobility

Cold War state of diplomatic hostility between the United States and the Soviet Union in the decades following World War II

fascism political movement that promotes extreme forms of nationalism, denial of individual rights, and dictatorial one-party rule

immigration entering and settling in a country of which one is not a native

imperialism policy in which a strong nation seeks to dominate other countries socially, economically, or politically

Industrial Revolution the shift from making goods by hand to making them by machine

industrialization development of industries for the machine production of goods

isolationism policy of avoiding political or military involvement with other countries

nationalism belief that people should be loyal mainly to their nation rather than to a king or an emperor

Nazism fascist policies of National Socialist German Workers' party, based on totalitarianism and belief in racial superiority

New Deal Franklin Roosevelt's economic reform program designed to solve the problems of the Great Depression

period a span of time, a number of years tied together by common elements

Reconstruction the period of rebuilding following the Civil War

segregation separation of people based on race

time line line that lists, in order, events and the dates on which they occurred

totalitarianism policy of government control over all aspects of public and private life

Part 2: Test-Taking Strategies and Practice

Multiple Choice

A multiple-choice question consists of a stem and a set of choices. The stem is usually in the form of a question or an incomplete sentence. One of the choices correctly answers the question or completes the sentence.

1 Read the stem carefully and try to answer the question or complete the sentence without looking at the choices.

2 Pay close attention to key words in the stem. They may direct you toward the correct answer.

3 Read each choice with the stem. Don't jump to conclusions about the correct answer until you've read all the choices.

4 Think carefully about questions that include *All of the above* among the choices.

5 After reading all of the choices, eliminate any that you know are incorrect.

6 Use modifiers to help narrow your choices further.

7 Look for the best answer among the remaining choices.

Improve your test-taking skills by practicing the strategies discussed in this section. Read the tips on each strategies page. Then apply them to the practice items on the two pages that follow. Use the Thinking Through the Answers page that follows the practice pages to help you evaluate your answers to the practice items.

World Geography Sample

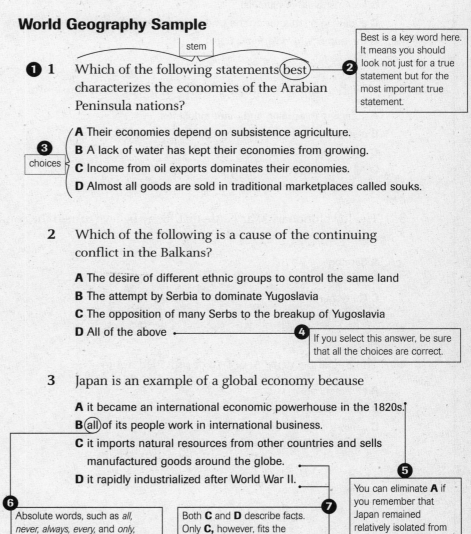

stem

1 **1** Which of the following statements best characterizes the economies of the Arabian Peninsula nations?

2 Best is a key word here. It means you should look not just for a true statement but for the most important true statement.

3 choices

A Their economies depend on subsistence agriculture.
B A lack of water has kept their economies from growing.
C Income from oil exports dominates their economies.
D Almost all goods are sold in traditional marketplaces called souks.

2 Which of the following is a cause of the continuing conflict in the Balkans?

A The desire of different ethnic groups to control the same land
B The attempt by Serbia to dominate Yugoslavia
C The opposition of many Serbs to the breakup of Yugoslavia
D All of the above

4 If you select this answer, be sure that all the choices are correct.

3 Japan is an example of a global economy because

A it became an international economic powerhouse in the 1820s.
B all of its people work in international business.
C it imports natural resources from other countries and sells manufactured goods around the globe.
D it rapidly industrialized after World War II.

6 Absolute words, such as *all, never, always, every,* and *only,* often signal an incorrect choice.

7 Both **C** and **D** describe facts. Only **C,** however, fits the definition of a global economy. Therefore, C is the best answer.

5 You can eliminate **A** if you remember that Japan remained relatively isolated from the West until 1853 when U.S. Commodore Perry arrived.

answers: 1 (C), 2 (D), 3 (C)

PRACTICE

United States History Sample

Directions: Read each question carefully and choose the *best* answer from the four alternatives.

1 Harriet Tubman was known best as

  A a slave who achieved her freedom.
  B an outspoken abolitionist.
  C a leading conductor on the Underground Railroad.
  D the author of *Uncle Tom's Cabin.*

2 Which of the following is considered a long-term cause of the Great Depression?

  A a decline in farming and other industries
  B a steady drop in consumer spending
  C a growing income gap
  D All of the above

3 The Revolutionary War battle that many believe turned the conflict in favor of the Americans was

  A Saratoga.
  B Yorktown.
  C Gettysburg.
  D Brandywine Creek.

4 The Social Security Act of 1935 provided aid to

  A all Americans.
  B senior citizens only.
  C seniors, poor families, and the unemployed.
  D business executives and entrepreneurs.

PRACTICE

World History Sample

Directions: Read each question carefully and choose the *best* answer from the four alternatives.

1 All of the following were considered factors that encouraged European exploration *except*

   A the search for greater wealth.
   B the desire to spread Christianity.
   C advances in sailing technology.
   D the invention of the printing press.

2 The powerful Spanish Navy, known as the Armada, met its defeat in 1588 at the hands of

   A the Swiss.
   B the Americans.
   C the English.
   D All of the above

3 By 1200, the Islam religion had spread from the Middle East to

   A all of Africa.
   B North Africa and Spain.
   C every continent except North America.
   D China and Japan.

4 The 19th century invention that revolutionized the world of communications was the

   A light bulb.
   B steel plow.
   C telephone.
   D computer.

ANSWERS

Thinking Through the Answers

QUESTIONS FROM PAGE 10:

1 **C** is correct. Tubman was *best* known for her work on the Underground Railroad.

  A and **B** are incorrect. Tubman was a freed slave and an outspoken abolitionist, but they are not what she was known for best.

  D is incorrect. Harriet Beecher Stowe wrote *Uncle Tom's Cabin*.

2 **D** is correct. Because all three distractors are long-term causes of the Depression, *All of the above* is the correct answer.

  A, B, and **C** are incorrect. Each of these is considered a cause of the Depression.

3 **A** is correct. The Americans' victory at Saratoga convinced the French to join their side and thus turned the tide of the war in favor of the colonists.

  B is incorrect. Yorktown was the final battle of the war.
  C is incorrect. Gettysburg was a battle fought during the Civil War.
  D is incorrect. The Americans lost the battle at Brandywine Creek.

4 **C** is correct. The Social Security Act helped this group of needy Americans.

  A and **B** are incorrect. Distractors with such absolute words as *all* or *only* usually signal an incorrect answer, as is the case here.

  D is incorrect. Business leaders and entrepreneurs most likely did not need government aid.

QUESTIONS FROM PAGE 11:

1 The word *except* signals that the question asks for something that was not a factor.

  D is correct. The printing press was not a factor in European exploration.
  A, B, and **C** are incorrect. All of the factors encouraged exploration.

2 **C** is correct. The English had a powerful navy at this time and competed with Spain for supremacy on the high seas.

  A is incorrect. Consider the location of Switzerland. It did not have a navy.
  B is incorrect. You should note the date of the Spanish Navy's defeat and realize that the American colonies had not yet been established.
  D is incorrect. If two of the first three distractors are incorrect, then *All of the above* cannot be correct.

3 B is correct. Islam spread to nearby North Africa and into Spain.

  A and **C** are incorrect. Distracters with such absolute words as *all* or *every* usually signal an incorrect answer, as is the case here.

  D is incorrect. It was more likely for Islam to spread to nearby North Africa and Spain than to the faraway lands of China and Japan.

4 **C** is correct. The telephone was a 19th-century communications device.

  A and **B** are incorrect. Neither of these are communications devices.
  D is incorrect. The question asks for a 19th-century invention, and the computer was invented in the 20th century.

Primary Sources

Primary sources are written or made by people who were at historical events, either as observers or participants. Primary sources include journals, diaries, letters, speeches, newspaper articles, autobiographies, wills, deeds, and financial records.

1 Look at the source line to learn about the document and its author. Consider the reliability of the information in the document.

2 Skim the document to get an idea of what it is about. (This source includes 3 paragraphs that address a related theme—rulers and moral behavior.)

3 Note any special punctuation. Ellipses, for example, indicate that words or sentences have been removed from the original.

4 Use active reading strategies. Ask and answer questions on the content as you read.

5 Use context clues to help you understand difficult or unfamiliar words. (From the context, you realize that *chastisements* means "punishments.")

6 Before rereading the document, skim the questions. This will help you focus your reading and more easily locate answers.

answers: 1 (B), 2 (C)

World History Sample

Moral Rulers

Book II, 3. The Master said, Govern the people by regulations, keep order among them by chastisements and they will flee from you, **5** and lose all self-respect. Govern them by moral force, keep order among them by ritual and they will keep their self-respect and come to you of their own accord (. .) **3**

Book XI, 23. . . . The Master said, . . . What I call a great minister is one who will only serve his prince while he can do so without infringement of the Way, and as soon as this is impossible, resigns. . . .

Book XIII, 6. The Master said, If the ruler himself is upright, all will go well even though he does not give orders. But if he himself is not upright, even though he gives orders, they will not be obeyed.

—*The Analects of Confucius*

> This is a collection of writings on government, ethics, literature, and other subjects by the ancient Chinese scholar and teacher Confucius. **1**

1 Which sentence *best* expresses the main idea shared by these paragraphs?

 A Rules and regulations are hard to live by.

 B Leaders should act morally in ruling the people.

 C A leader's goodness is judged by the punishments he administers.

 D Rulers should expect their people to obey them no matter what they say.

2 This advice from Confucius seems most appropriate for

 A workers and farmers.

 B merchants and town artisans.

 C rulers and their advisers.

 D soldiers and priests.

PRACTICE

United States History Sample

Directions: Below is an excerpt from a 1900 speech by presidential candidate William Jennings Bryan. His subject is the U.S. annexation of the Philippines after the Spanish-American War. Use this passage and your knowledge of U.S. history to answer the questions.

A colonial policy means that we shall send to the Philippine Islands a few traders, a few taskmasters, and a few officeholders, and an army large enough to support the authority of a small fraction of the people while they rule the natives.

If we have an imperial policy we must have a great standing army as its natural and necessary complement. . . . A large standing army is not only a pecuniary [financial] burden to the people and, if accompanied by compulsory service, a constant source of irritation but is even more a menace to a republican form of government. The army is the personification of force, and militarism will inevitably change the ideals of the people and turn the thoughts of our young men from the arts of peace to the science of war. . . .

Some argue that American rule in the Philippine Islands will result in the better education of the Filipinos. Be not deceived. If we expect to maintain a colonial policy, we shall not find it to our advantage to educate the people. The educated Filipinos are now in revolt against, and the most ignorant ones have made the least resistance to our dominion. If we are to govern them without their consent and give them no voice in determining the taxes which they must pay, we dare not educate them lest they learn to read the Declaration of Independence and the Constitution of the United States and mock us for our inconsistency.

—William Jennings Bryan, quoted in *The Annals of America*

1   Which of the following groups would Bryan's speech have appealed to the most?

   A imperialists

   B farmers

   C bankers

   D anti-imperialists

2   What is Bryan's objection to a large standing army?

   A It would lead to the dissolution of the arts.

   B It would place a pecuniary, or financial, burden on the Filipinos.

   C It would make America more militaristic and war-like.

   D All of the above

3   Which of the following is the most accurate definition of the word *ignorant?*

   A polite

   B uneducated

   C angry

   D healthy

4   The colonization of the Philippines appeared to be most inconsistent with what idea promoted by the Declaration of Independence and the U.S. Constitution?

   A the right to self-government

   B the right to free health care

   C the right to employment

   D the right to due process

Name _____ Date _____

PRACTICE

World Geography Sample

Directions: Below is an excerpt from the observations of Christopher Columbus upon his arrival in modern-day Cuba in 1492. Use this passage and your knowledge of world geography to answer the questions.

I saw a large stream of very fine water, which descended from a mountain and made a great noise. I went to the river and saw in it some stone, glittering like gold. . . . It appeared to me that there certainly must be gold here, and I ordered certain of those stones to be gathered for the Sovereigns. . . . I went to the mouth of the river, and at the foot of that cape on the SE side I entered a bay which was very large and deep and which could contain 100 ships without lines or anchors. Eyes have never seen such a harbor. The mountain ranges are very high, from which many fine streams descend; all of the ranges are covered with pines; and everywhere there are the most varied and beautiful groves of trees. . . . I just cannot express to you, my Sovereigns, what a joy and pleasure it is to see all this, especially the pines, because there could be built here as many ships as desired, simply by bringing the necessary implements—except the wood and fish, of which there are enormous quantities.

—from the *Log of Christopher Columbus*

1   Which of following statements most accurately describes the geography of Cuba?

   A It was mostly flat.
   B It was dry and barren.
   C It was densely forested.
   D It was landlocked.

2   Which of following statements reveals that Columbus was delighted with the land of Cuba?

   A "I saw a large stream of very fine water."
   B "I entered a bay . . . which could contain 100 ships without lines or anchors."
   C "Everywhere there are the most varied and beautiful groves of trees."
   D All of the above

3   Which of the following statements most accurately describes what Columbus would do with Cuba's forestland?

   A leave it untouched
   B use its trees for building purposes
   C clear it to create farmland
   D collect the sap from the trees to make syrup

4   Columbus was most impressed with Cuba's

   A climate.
   B people.
   C streams.
   D natural resources.

ANSWERS

Thinking Through the Answers

Questions from Page 14:

1 The main idea of Bryan's speech is that annexation of the Philippines was wrong.

D is correct. Anti-imperialists would have been supportive of his speech.

A is incorrect. Bryan's ideas would not have appealed to an imperialist.

B and **C** are incorrect. It is not known if farmers and bankers supported Bryan's views.

2 **C** is correct. Bryan fears a larger army will turn people's thoughts to war.

A is incorrect. The "arts of peace" have nothing to do with "cultural arts."

B is incorrect. Bryan refers to the American taxpayers' financial burden of supporting an enlarged military force.

D is incorrect. If **A** and **B** are incorrect, then *All of the above* cannot be correct.

3 The speaker is making a comparison between *educated* and *ignorant,* which means that the two terms are somehow related.

B is correct. If the terms *educated* and *ignorant* are related, then uneducated seems the most accurate definition of *ignorant.*

A, C, and **D** are incorrect. The terms *polite, angry,* or *healthy* are not related to the word *educated.*

4 **A** is correct. Recall that both the Declaration of Independence and U.S. Constitution advocate self-government.

B and **C** are incorrect. Neither of these issues is referred to in the Declaration or the Constitution.

D is incorrect. The right of due process is guaranteed in the U.S. Constitution, but not mentioned in the Declaration.

Questions from Page 15:

1 **C** is correct. Columbus mentions mountain ranges "covered with pines."

A is incorrect. Columbus mentions mountain ranges.

B is incorrect. The mention of rivers and trees indicates a fertile land.

D is incorrect. Knowing that Cuba is an island eliminates this distractor.

2 **D** is correct. **A, B,** and **C** are all possible answers, so *All of the above* is the correct answer.

A, B, and **C** are incorrect. All these statements indicate how impressed Columbus is with Cuba.

3 **B** is correct. Columbus suggests using the trees to build ships.

A is incorrect. Columbus suggests using pine trees to build ships, not leaving the land untouched.

C and **D** are incorrect. Columbus makes no mention of clearing the land for farming or collecting sap.

4 **D** is correct. Columbus was impressed with all of Cuba's natural resources.

A and **B** are incorrect. Columbus doesn't mention Cuba's climate or people.

C is incorrect. Columbus was impressed with many aspects of Cuba besides streams.

Secondary Sources

Secondary sources are descriptions of places, people, cultures, and events. Usually, secondary sources are made by people who are not directly involved in the event or living in the place being discussed.

The most common types of written secondary sources are textbooks, reference books, some magazine and newspaper articles, and biographies.

❶ Read the title to preview the content of the passage.

❷ Look at the source line to learn more about the document and its origin. (The spelling of the word *organized* indicates that the magazine is probably from Great Britain.)

❸ Look for topic sentences. Ask yourself what the main idea is.

❹ As you read, use context clues to guess at the meaning of difficult or unfamiliar words. (Use the description of crime in the passage to understand that the word *pervasiveness* most likely means "being everywhere.")

❺ Read actively by asking and answering questions about the passage.

❻ Before rereading the passage, skim the questions to identify the information you need to find.

World Geography Sample

❶ Organized Crime in Russia

❸ This highlights the key feature of Russian criminality: its **❹** (pervasiveness) "Organised crime usually deals with [minor] economic issues . . . [but] in Russia it's the mainstream," notes Toby Latta of Control Risks, a London security [firm]. Russian criminality reaches the highest levels of government—is, indeed, often indistinguishable from it. And it affects the humblest activity. Buy a jar of coffee? More likely than not, you are feeding organised crime: according to a grumbling Nestlé, most coffee sold in Russia has evaded full import duties. Give money to a beggar? He will have paid the local mafia for his spot on the street. Build a factory? You will pay one lot of bureaucrats to get it going, another to keep it running. In Russia, organised crime and corruption are everywhere. **❸**

> You might ask: What makes organized crime in Russia different from organized crime in other countries? Are crime and corruption in all levels of society new to Russian culture? **❺**

> The last sentence restates the main idea.

❷ Excerpt from "Russian (Organised) Crime," from *The Economist,* August 28, 1999. Copyright © 1998 The Economist. Reprinted by permission.

1 What is the main idea of this passage?

A The Russian economy is in a depression.

B The Russian government is ineffective.

C Organized crime operates in all areas of the Russian economy.

D Russia is on the verge of collapse.

❻

2 Which of the following conclusions can you draw from this passage?

A Anyone who wants to start a business in Russia may have to pay the mafia first.

B The Russian government loses money because some import taxes are not paid.

C The Russian mafia operates within the government.

D All of the above

answers: 1 (C), 2 (D)

PRACTICE

United States History Sample

Directions: Use this passage about the nullification crisis during the presidency of Andrew Jackson and your knowledge of U.S. history to answer the questions.

The Nullification Crisis

President Jackson confronted head-on the growing sectional crisis . . . over the issue of states' rights [versus] the federal Union. At a dinner in 1830 marking the eighty-seventh anniversary of Thomas Jefferson's birth, Jackson offered a toast: "Our Federal Union—it must be preserved!" Vice President [John] Calhoun, who was the principal advocate of the South's right to nullify federal laws, responded with a counter-toast: "The Union—next to our liberty the most dear!" Thus the lines were drawn. In 1832, Jackson signed into law a moderate tariff, less exacting than the Tariff of Abominations [a tariff criticized by Southerners as too burdensome]. This failed to satisfy South Carolina, which quickly enacted the Ordinance of Nullification declaring the tariff null and void in that state. Within weeks Jackson responded with a strongly worded proclamation warning South Carolina to comply with the tariff law and denouncing the doctrine of nullification as "uncompatible with the existence of the Union." . . . To further demonstrate his determination, Jackson obtained from Congress the power to use armed force to collect import duties. The crisis ended with passage of the Tariff of 1833, a compromise bill sponsored by Senator Henry Clay and acceptable to both Jackson and the South.

—William A. Degregorio, *The Complete Book of U.S. Presidents*

1 What was Andrew Jackson's attitude toward the principle of states' rights?

A He supported it.

B He opposed it.

C He had no opinion about it.

D He favored it under some circumstances.

2 You can infer from this passage that an important part of South Carolina's economy was

A banking.

B industry.

C the purchasing of imported goods.

D trade with the Native Americans.

3 During his political career, Henry Clay earned the nickname

A the Great Compromiser.

B the Great Communicator.

C the Great Divider.

D Old Hickory.

4 The nullification crisis foreshadowed an even greater crisis regarding states' rights that ultimately led to the

A Revolutionary War.

B War of 1812.

C Civil War.

D Mexican-American War.

PRACTICE

World History Sample

Directions: Use this passage about Russia's efforts in World War I and your knowledge of world history to answer the questions.

Russia's War Effort Collapses

During the first several years of the war, perhaps no combatant struggled as badly as Russia. Unlike the nations of western Europe, Russia had yet to become industrialized. As a result, the Russian army was continually short on food, guns, ammunition, clothes, boots, and blankets. The Russian army had only one asset—its numbers. Throughout the war the Russian army suffered enormous battlefield losses—more than 2 million soldiers killed, wounded, or captured in 1915 alone—and yet the army continually rebuilt its ranks. Despite all its difficulties, the Russian army managed to tie up hundreds of thousands of German troops in the east for more than three years.

By spring 1917, however, civil unrest in Russia—due in part to war-related shortages of food and fuel—had brought the czar's government to the brink of collapse. Faced with the prospect of revolution, Czar Nicholas abdicated his throne on March 15. A provisional government was established, and its leaders vowed to continue the war effort. However, the war-weary Russian army—having suffered some 5 million casualties thus far—refused to fight any longer. In November 1917, the Communists seized power and insisted on ending Russia's involvement in the war. In March 1918, Russia and Germany signed the Treaty of Brest-Litovsk, which ended the war between them. As a result, Germany was able to send nearly all of its forces to the Western Front and launch a massive attack on the Allies in France.

1 The Russian war effort collapsed due to

   A a continual lack of supplies and weapons.

   B a war-weariness on the part of Russian soldiers.

   C growing civil unrest brought on by war-related shortages.

   D All of the above

2 You can infer from this passage that Russia had

   A many factories.

   B a large population.

   C fertile farm land.

   D long and cold winters.

3 Based on this passage, Russia's importance to the Allied war effort was its ability to

   A defeat the German U-boat fleet.

   B defeat the Germans on the Eastern Front.

   C provide the Allies with weapons and other supplies.

   D keep Germany from focusing solely on the Western Front.

4 Which of the following statements best summarizes this passage?

   A As war-related turmoil gripped Russia, the Communists seized power.

   B Despite its many hardships, the Russian army battled the Germans for years.

   C The war led to the downfall of Czar Nicholas.

   D A war-weary Russia withdrew from the conflict and raised Germany's war hopes.

ANSWERS

Thinking Through the Answers

Questions from Page 18:

1 **B** is correct. By examining Jackson's quotes and actions against South Carolina, you should determine that the president opposed states' rights.

A, C, and **D** are incorrect. Jackson refers to states' rights as a threat to the Union.

2 **C** is correct. The fact that South Carolina expressed opposition to high tariffs, a tax on imported items, most likely meant that purchasing imports was an important part of its economy.

A and **B** are incorrect. Banking and industry were hallmarks of the northern economy, as the South had few factories or financial centers.

D is incorrect. There is no reference in the passage to trade with Native Americans.

3 **A** is correct. Recall Clay's efforts to end the nullification crisis and his key role in settling other divisive issues during the years leading up to the Civil War.

B is incorrect. This is the nickname of President Ronald Reagan.

C is incorrect. Such a nickname is the opposite of how Clay acted.

D is incorrect. This nickname belonged to Andrew Jackson.

4 The word *foreshadow* indicates something to come.

C is correct. The Civil War took place about 20 years after the nullification crisis and involved the issue of states' rights.

A, B, and **D** are incorrect. The Revolutionary War and the War of 1812 happened before the nullification crisis, and the Mexican-American War took place some years after the nullification crisis.

Questions from Page 19:

1 **D** is correct. **A, B,** and **C** are all possible answers, so *All of the above* is the correct answer.

2 **B** is correct. The fact that Russia could continually rebuild the ranks of its army suggests the country had an enormous population.

A is incorrect. The passage states that Russia had yet to become industrialized, which means that the nation most likely had very few factories.

C and **D** are incorrect. Neither of these characteristics is discussed in this passage.

3 **D** is correct. Upon Russia's withdrawal Germany quickly moved its forces from the Eastern Front to the Western Front.

A is incorrect. The passage makes no mention of U-boats or the war at sea.

B is incorrect. The Russians surrendered to the Germans.

C is incorrect. The Russians were unable to supply their own forces, and thus were most likely unable to supply the Allies with any materials.

4 The main topic of the passage is the causes and consequences of Russia's withdrawal from the war.

D is correct. This statement provides the reasons for and effects of Russia's withdrawal.

A, B, and **C** are incorrect. Each of these statements summarizes smaller events and does not make the best overall summary.

Political Cartoons

Political cartoons use a combination of words and images to express a point of view on political issues. They are useful primary sources, because they reflect the opinions of the time.

1 Identify the subject of the cartoon. Titles and captions often provide clues to the subject matter.

2 Use labels to help identify the people, places, and events represented in the cartoon.

3 Note where and when the cartoon was published for more information on people, places, and events.

4 Identify any important symbols—ideas or images that stand for something else—in the cartoon.

5 Analyze the point of view presented in the cartoon. The use of caricature—the exaggeration of physical features—often signals how the cartoonist feels.

6 Interpret the cartoonist's message.

World History Sample

1 **"NEXT!"**

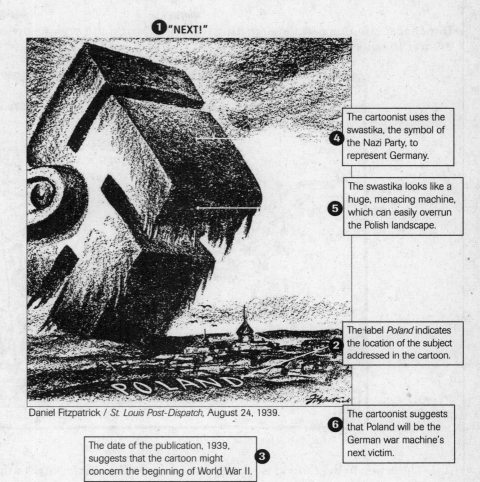

4 The cartoonist uses the swastika, the symbol of the Nazi Party, to represent Germany.

5 The swastika looks like a huge, menacing machine, which can easily overrun the Polish landscape.

2 The label *Poland* indicates the location of the subject addressed in the cartoon.

Daniel Fitzpatrick / *St. Louis Post-Dispatch*, August 24, 1939.

6 The cartoonist suggests that Poland will be the German war machine's next victim.

3 The date of the publication, 1939, suggests that the cartoon might concern the beginning of World War II.

1 The machine-like swastika in the cartoon represents

A Nazi Germany.

B the Soviet Union.

C Napoleon's empire.

D the Polish military.

2 Which sentence *best* summarizes the cartoonist's message?

A Germany must beware of Poland.

B Poland is in danger of civil war.

C Germany and Poland are military giants.

D Poland will be Germany's next victim.

answers: 1 (A); 2 (D)

PRACTICE

World Geography Sample

Directions: Use this cartoon depicting life in the 1970s and your knowledge of world geography to answer the questions below.

WELL WELL WELL.
LET ME GUESS.
WORLD'S ONLY SUPERPOWER, IS IT?

OPEC PRICED DAILY

I NEVER FORGET A POSTURE.

TOLES ©2001 THE NEW REPUBLIC

Toles, *The Buffalo News*, 2001

1 The action in the cartoon is taking place in

A China.
B South America.
C the United States.
D the Middle East.

2 The figure crawling along the sand is meant to represent

A Germany.
B Russia.
C the United States.
D Saudi Arabia.

3 In the view of the cartoonist, the United States

A should join OPEC.
B is too reliant on foreign sources for its energy.
C consumes only a moderate amount of energy.
D has developed plenty of alternative fuel sources.

4 One way that Americans could address the problem presented in this cartoon is

A to walk or ride bicycles more often.
B to drive bigger cars.
C to stop carpooling to work.
D All of the above

PRACTICE

United States History Sample

Directions: Use the cartoon and your knowledge of U.S. history to answer the questions below.

Cy Hungerford, *Pittsburgh Post-Gazette,* April 1950

1   According to the top frame, Americans feared that President Truman

   A was too small to be president.

   B would act too much like Franklin Roosevelt.

   C would be unable to match Roosevelt's grand and heroic feats.

   D lacked the proper taste and style to be president.

2   The bottom frame of the cartoon depicts Truman as

   A a good athlete.

   B a successful politician.

   C an inactive president.

   D a poor imitation of Roosevelt.

3   The cartoonist's view of Truman is

   A favorable.

   B unfavorable.

   C indifferent.

   D too difficult to determine.

4   Which of the following would make the most fitting title for this cartoon?

   A Stuck in FDR's Shadow

   B The Do-Nothing President

   C Our Greatest Leader

   D Blazing His Own Trail

ANSWERS

Thinking Through the Answers

Questions from Page 22:

1 **D** is correct. OPEC, which is represented by the gas station in the cartoon, has members from the oil-rich countries of the Middle East.

A, B, and **C** are incorrect.

2 **C** is correct. The image of Uncle Sam clearly denotes the United States.

A, B, and **D** are incorrect. The figure is Uncle Sam, which represents the United States, not Germany, Russia, or Saudi Arabia.

3 **B** is the correct answer. By depicting a desperate Uncle Sam crawling to OPEC with an empty gas can, the cartoonist clearly believes the United States relies too heavily on foreign oil.

A is incorrect. The scene does not address OPEC membership.
C is incorrect. The cartoonist believes that the nation consumes too much energy.
D is incorrect. If the United States developed alternative fuel sources, it wouldn't be so reliant on OPEC.

4 **A** is correct. By walking or biking, Americans can reduce gasoline consumption.

B and **C** are incorrect. Both of these measures would increase gasoline consumption.
D is incorrect. If two of the distractors are incorrect, then *All of the above* is not correct.

Questions from Page 23:

1 Someone who leaves "big shoes to fill" has achieved a high level of success that any followers are expected to continue.

C is correct. The metaphor of Truman's inability to fill Roosevelt's shoes relays the message that Truman won't be able to measure up to his predecessor.
A and **D** are incorrect.
B is incorrect. The scene shows Americans fear that Truman won't be able to take after Roosevelt.

2 **B** is correct. The obstacle signifies a political hurdle, and Truman's ability to leap it demonstrates political skill.

A is incorrect. Truman's skill is political not athletic.
C is incorrect. The scene depicts Truman as an active and robust president.
D is incorrect. The cartoonist shows Truman has developed a style all his own.

3 **A** is correct. The cartoonist shows his favorable opinion of the president by depicting Truman as a strong and successful politician.

B and **C** are incorrect. The cartoonist appears to hold a favorable view of Truman.
D is incorrect. By showing Truman unsure and nervous in the top frame and happy and confident in the second frame, the cartoonist conveys his view in a clear and concise manner.

4 **D** is correct. The main message of this cartoon is that Truman stepped out from the shadow of Roosevelt to become his own man and a successful leader.

A and **B** are incorrect. The cartoonist depicts Truman in an active and aggressive pose.
C is incorrect. The cartoonist offers no comparisons between Truman and other presidents.

Charts

Charts present information in a visual form. Geography textbooks use several types of charts, including tables, flow charts, Venn diagrams, and infographics. The type of chart most commonly found in tests is the table, which organizes information in columns and rows for easy viewing.

❶ Read the title to identify the broad subject of the chart.

❷ Read the column and row headings and any other labels. The headings and labels will provide more details on the subject of the chart.

❸ Compare and contrast the information from column to column and row to row.

❹ Try to draw conclusions from the information in the chart. Ask yourself: What trends or patterns does the chart show?

❺ Read the questions and then study the chart again.

World Geography Sample

❶ Adult Literacy Rates in South Asia by Gender, 1995

❷ Country	Male	Female	Total
Bangladesh	49%	26%	38%
Bhutan	56%	28%	42%
India	66%	38%	52%
Maldives	93%	93%	93%
Nepal	41%	14%	28%
Sri Lanka	93%	87%	90%
Pakistan	50%	24%	38%

❹ Based on the data in this chart, you might conclude that males in most of these countries receive more education than females.

Sources: World Health Organization; CIA, *The World Fact Book 2000*

❸ Compare and contrast the literacy rates of males and females in each country.

1 What is the general pattern in the literacy rates for males and females of this region?

A The rates for males and females are similar.

B The rates for males are generally much higher than those for females.

C The rates for females are generally much higher than those for males.

D The rates for both sexes are extremely low in all the countries.

2 One observation that you can make about the literacy rate in these countries is that the

A higher the female literacy rate is, the higher the total literacy rate is.

B higher the literacy rate, the less interest females have in reading and writing.

C literacy rate in mountainous countries is higher than the rate in island countries.

D lower the total literacy rate is, the higher the female literacy rate is.

answers: 1 (B), 2 (A)

Name _____   Date _____

United States History Sample

Directions: Use the chart and your knowledge of U.S. history to answer the questions below.

Characteristics of College Freshman

Characteristic	1970	1980	1990
Sex			
Male	55%	49%	46%
Female	45%	51%	54%
Average Grade in High School			
A	16%	21%	23%
B	58%	60%	58%
C	27%	19%	19%
D	1%	1%	0%
Political Orientation			
Liberal	34%	20%	23%
Middle of the Road	45%	60%	55%
Conservative	17%	17%	20%
Probable of Field of Study			
Arts and Humanities	16%	9%	9%
Biological Sciences	4%	4%	4%
Business	16%	24%	21%
Education	11%	7%	10%
Engineering	9%	12%	8%
Physical Science	2%	3%	2%
Social Science	17%	7%	10%

Source: U.S. Bureau of the Census, *Statistical Abstract of the United States: 1993*, Washington D.C. 1993, p. 180

1 Between 1970 and 1990, the percentage of female college freshmen

A increased.
B decreased.
C stayed the same.
D remained less than the percentage of male freshmen.

2 Between 1970 and 1990, college freshmen in general

A did worse academically in high school.
B did better academically in high school.
C exhibited no change academically in high school.
D studied longer hours in high school.

3 If the trend for 1980 and 1990 continued, the year 2000 would show an increased percentage of college freshmen entering the field of

A arts and humanities.
B biological sciences.
C education.
D business.

4 The chart exemplifies what trend of the late 20th century?

A College freshmen were more conservative than liberal.
B More women than men attended college.
C College freshmen were not interested in business studies.
D More high school students were attending college.

PRACTICE

World History and World Geography Sample

Directions: Use the chart and your knowledge of world history and geography to answer the questions below.

A Comparison of Asian Countries, 1984

Nations	Land Area (sq. miles)	Population (thousands)	Unemployment (% of workforce)	Defense Spending (% of federal budget)
Japan	145,870	120,083	2.7	5.4
Philippines	115,800	53,351	7.0	9.5
South Korea	38,279	40,496	3.8	26.6
Taiwan	13,900	19,031	2.4	44.7
Singapore	240	2,529	2.7	20.9

Source: Kurina, George Thomas, *The New Book of World Rankings;* B.R. Mitchell, *International Historical Statistics.*

1 The country with the highest population density, or persons per square mile, is

A Japan.

B Singapore.

C the Philippines.

D Taiwan.

2 In which country would it probably be most difficult to find a job?

A Japan

B Taiwan

C Philippines

D South Korea

3 The countries that spend more than a quarter of their national budget on defense are

A Japan and the Philippines.

B Taiwan and Japan.

C Singapore and South Korea.

D Taiwan and South Korea.

4 Taiwan spends such a large portion of its budget on defense most likely due to its hostile relationship with neighboring

A India.

B China.

C Vietnam.

D North Korea.

ANSWERS

Thinking Through the Answers

Questions from Page 26:

1 **A** is correct. The percentage of female freshmen increased during this period.
   B and **C** are incorrect. The percentage of female college freshmen neither decreased nor remained constant.
   D is incorrect. By 1980 females were a greater percentage of college freshmen.

2 **B** is correct. Between 1970 and 1990, the percentage of "A" range high school students increased, while the percentage of those in the "C" and "D" ranges decreased.
   A is incorrect. The chart shows an increase, not a decrease.
   C is incorrect. The chart does indicate academic change.
   D is incorrect. This chart does not address this topic.

3 **C** is correct. The chart shows an increase in 1990 over 1980. Should that trend continue, the percentage would be even greater in 2000.
   A and **B** are incorrect. The percentage of students entering these fields of study remained the same for 1980 and 1990. If that trend continued for the year 2000, there would be no increase.
   D is incorrect. The percentage of students entering the business field in 1990 was less than in 1980. If the trend continued, the year 2000 would show a decrease.

4 **B** is correct. Women outnumbered men slightly in 1980 and by an even greater number ten years later.
   A is incorrect. The percentage of liberal college freshmen continuously outnumbered those who saw themselves as conservatives.
   C is incorrect. Business was the most popular field of study shown on the chart.
   D is incorrect. There are no statistics on college enrollment.

Questions from Page 27:

1 Population density is figured by dividing the total population of a country by its total land area.
   B is correct. Singapore's population density is about 10,537 persons per square mile, the highest of the nations listed on the chart.
   A, C, and **D** are incorrect. Japan's population density is roughly 823 persons per square mile, the Philippines has about 460 persons per square mile, and Taiwan has about 1,367 persons per square mile.

2 A person probably would have the most difficulty finding a job in the country with the highest unemployment rate.
   C is correct. The Philippines has the highest unemployment rate.
   A, B, and **D** are incorrect. Japan and Taiwan have the lowest unemployment rates of the nations listed on the chart, and South Korea's unemployment rate is about half of the rate of unemployment in the Philippines.

3 A quarter equals 25 percent.
   D is correct. The only two nations listed on the chart that spend more than 25 percent of their budget on defense are Taiwan and South Korea.
   A, B, and **C** are incorrect. Japan and the Philippines spend less than 10 percent. Taiwan spends over 25 percent. South Korea spends just over a quarter of its budget on defense, but Singapore spends only about 20 percent.

4 **B** is correct. Taiwan sits just off the coast of China. Recall that the two nations share tense relations over the issue of Taiwan's sovereignty.
   A is incorrect. Taiwan lies just east of the Asian mainland, while India is located in South Asia, and thus cannot be considered a neighbor.
   C is incorrect. Vietnam is located across the China Sea from Taiwan, and the two countries are not outwardly hostile toward one another.
   D is incorrect. North Korea is not a neighbor of Taiwan, but of South Korea.

Line and Bar Graphs

Graphs show statistics in a visual form. Line graphs are particularly useful for showing changes over time. Bar graphs make it easy to compare numbers or sets of numbers.

1 Read the title and identify the broad subject of the graph.

2 Study the labels on the vertical and horizontal axes to see the kinds of information presented in the graph. Note the intervals between amounts and between dates. This will help you read the graph more efficiently.

3 Look at the source line and evaluate the reliability of the information in the graph.

4 If the graph presents information over time, look for trends—generalizations you can make about changes over time.

5 Draw conclusions and make inferences based on information in the graph.

6 Read the questions carefully and then study the graph again.

World History Sample

1 Exports of English Manufactured Goods, 1699–1774

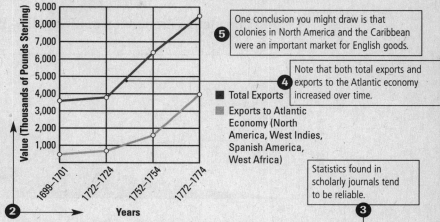

One conclusion you might draw is that colonies in North America and the Caribbean were an important market for English goods. **5**

Note that both total exports and exports to the Atlantic economy increased over time. **4**

■ Total Exports

▨ Exports to Atlantic Economy (North America, West Indies, Spanish America, West Africa)

Statistics found in scholarly journals tend to be reliable. **3**

Source: R. Davis, "English Foreign Trade, 1700–1774," *Economic History Review* (1962)

6 1 Which statement *best* describes the change in proportion of Atlantic economy exports to total exports?

A It started small and remained small.

B It started large and remained large.

C It grew over time.

D It decreased over time.

1 Nations with High Foreign Debt, 1998

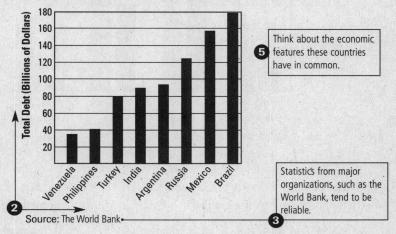

Think about the economic features these countries have in common. **5**

Statistics from major organizations, such as the World Bank, tend to be reliable. **3**

Source: The World Bank

6 2 Which nation has the largest foreign debt?

A Venezuela

B Brazil

C Mexico

D Russia

answers: 1 (C), 2 (B)

PRACTICE

World Geography Sample

Directions: Use the graphs and your knowledge of U.S. geography to answer the questions below.

Cumulative Production of CFCs: 1958–1994

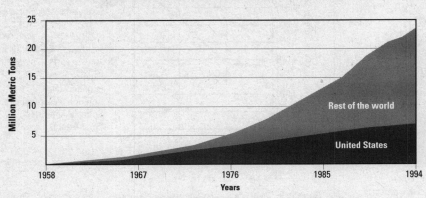

Source: U.S. International Trade Commission, *Synthetic Organic Chemicals, United States Production and Sales* (U.S. GPO, 1994 and various years).

Population: 2000–2050

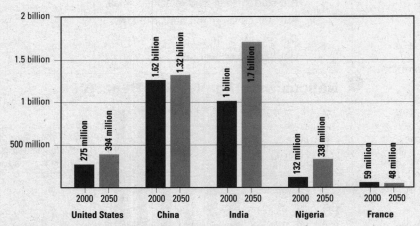

Source: *The World Almanac and Book of Facts 2001*

1 Which of the following statements is NOT true according to the graph?

A From 1958 to 1994, annual U.S. production of CFCs never surpassed 10 million tons.

B In 1985, the United States accounted for about a third of the world's CFC production.

C In 1994, the United States produced more CFCs than all other nations combined.

D From 1985 and 1994, world production of CFCs increased by almost 10 million tons.

2 Which of the following statements is true according to the graph?

A The most populated country listed on the graph will have the largest population by 2050.

B By 2050, more people will live in India than all of Europe.

C At its current growth rate, India's population will exceed 2 billion by 2100.

D The trend of these nations indicates that the world's population is decreasing.

Name _____ Date _____

United States History Sample

Directions: Use the graphs and your knowledge of U.S. history to answer the questions below.

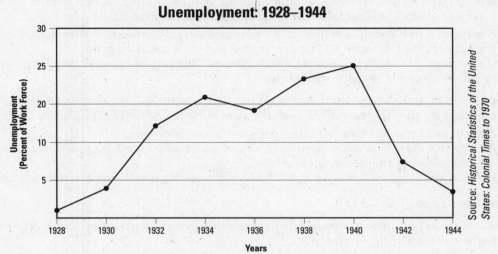

Unemployment: 1928–1944

Source: *Historical Statistics of the United States: Colonial Times to 1970*

1 Between what years did the unemployment rate increase the most?

A 1928–1930
B 1930–1932
C 1936–1938
D 1940–1942

2 The major historical event that played a key role in helping to end the nation's Depression-era unemployment was

A World War II.
B the Red Scare.
C the Cold War.
D Black Tuesday.

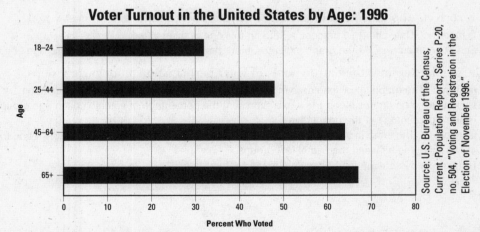

Voter Turnout in the United States by Age: 1996

Source: U.S. Bureau of the Census, Current Population Reports, Series P-20, no. 504, "Voting and Registration in the Election of November 1996."

3 In which age group did about half of the members vote?

A 18–24
B 25–44
C 45–64
D 65 and over

4 Which of the following statements is true according to the graph?

A In 1996, almost 70 percent of Americans were 65 or older.
B The increase in voter participation was greatest from 45-64 to 65 and older.
C The older people were, the more likely they were to vote.
D Voters under the age of 18 were not taken into account.

ANSWERS

Thinking Through the Answers

Questions from Page 30:

1 **B** is correct. In 1985, the world produced about 15 million tons of CFCs and the United States produced about 5 million tons—or roughly a third of the total.

A is incorrect. By following 10 million ton line, you can see that U.S. production never reached that amount.

C is incorrect. The U.S. output of CFCs was less than that of the rest of the world.

D is incorrect. The world's CFC output between 1985 and 1994 increased from 15 million to nearly 25 million tons, an increase of almost 10 million tons.

2 **C** is correct. India's population increased by about 700 million between 2000 and 2050. If it increases by another 700 million over the same time period, it would hit about 2.4 billion.

A is incorrect. China, not India, is the most populated country on the graph.

B is incorrect. There is no way to determine this information from the graph because France is the only European country represented on the graph.

D is incorrect. Except for France, the trend of these nations indicates an increase in world population.

QUESTIONS FROM PAGE 31:

1 **B** is correct. The unemployment rate between these years increased by about 15 percent, the highest jump depicted on the chart.

A is incorrect. The graph indicates a roughly 5 percent increase.

C is incorrect. The rate increase between these two years is about 2 percent.

D is incorrect. These two years represent the sharpest *decrease* in the rate.

2 A is correct. World War II began toward the end of 1939 and helped to ease the nation's unemployment by creating numerous war-related jobs.

B is incorrect. The Red Scare occurred in the 1920s, before the Great Depression.

C is incorrect. The Cold War began long after the Great Depression.

D is incorrect. Black Tuesday was the day of the stock market crash in 1929, an event that was a factor in the Great Depression and its massive unemployment.

3 **B** is correct. About 50 percent or half of the members in this age bracket voted.

A is incorrect. Only about 30 percent, a third, in this age bracket voted.

C and D are incorrect. As the graph indicates, more than half of the members of these age brackets voted.

4 The graph examines the narrow topic of voter participation among age groups.

C is correct. The graph show increases in the length of each bar showing voter participation.

A is incorrect. The figures along the x-axis represent the percentage of voters in each age group, not each group's percentage of the population.

B is incorrect. The jump in voter participation percentages is greater from 18–24 to 25–44 and from 25–44 to 45–64 than it is between the two oldest groups.

D is incorrect. No one under 18 can vote in the United States.

Pie Graphs

A pie, or circle, graph shows relationships among the parts of a whole. These parts look like slices of a pie. The size of each slice is proportional to the percentage of the whole that it represents.

1 Read the title and identify the broad subject of the pie graph.

2 Look at the legend to see what each of the slices of the pie represents.

3 Read the source line and note the origin of the data shown in the pie graph.

4 Compare the slices of the pie, and try to make generalizations and draw conclusions from your comparisons.

5 Read the questions carefully and review difficult terms.

6 Think carefully about questions that have *not* in the stem.

7 Eliminate choices that you know are wrong.

World Geography Sample

1 **Typical Growing Season Work Day for 10-Year-Old Girl in Rural Nepal**

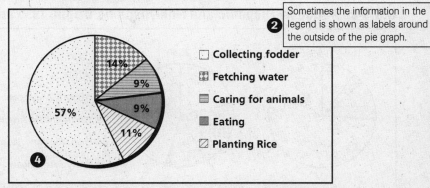

2 Sometimes the information in the legend is shown as labels around the outside of the pie graph.

4

57% 14% 9% 9% 11%

- Collecting fodder
- Fetching water
- Caring for animals
- Eating
- Planting Rice

3 **Source:** Adapted from "A working day in the life of a 10-year old girl in Nepal," from *Listening to Smaller Voices* by Victoria Johnson, Joanna Hill, and Edda Ivan-Smith. Copyright © 1995 by ActionAid Nepal. Reprinted by permission.

1 A typical 10-year-old girl in rural Nepal spends the greatest percentage of her time

A planting rice.

B eating.

C collecting fodder. **5** The word *fodder* refers to feed for livestock. It is usually coarsely chopped straw or hay.

D fetching water.

6

2 Which of the following is *not* a conclusion you can draw from the information in this pie graph?

A Young girls spend no time raising animals in rural Nepal.

B During the growing season, children in rural Nepal do farm chores most of the day.

C Rice is an important part of the diet in Nepal.

D Children in Nepal do not attend school during the growing season.

7 You can eliminate **B** because the pie graph shows they do spend most of their day doing farm chores.

answers: 1 (A), 2 (D)

PRACTICE

United States History Sample

Directions: Use the pie graphs and your knowledge of U.S. history to answer the questions below.

U.S. Population by Hispanic and Non-Hispanic Origin, 1995 and 2050 (Projected)

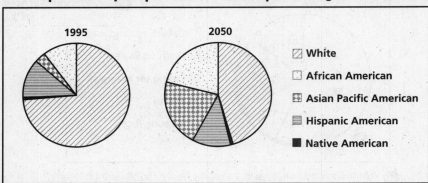

Source: Larry Shinagawa and Michael Jang, *Atlas of American Diversity*

1 Which group more than doubled its percentage of the population?

   A whites
   B African Americans
   C Native Americans
   D Hispanic Americans

2 Hispanic Americans will surpass which group in terms of percentage of the overall population?

   A whites
   B African Americans
   C Asian Pacific Americans
   D Native Americans

3 The projected population changes between 1995 and 2050 are due in part to a wave of immigration in recent decades from

   A Europe.
   B Canada.
   C Latin America.
   D the Middle East.

4 If the projections for 2050 prove right, which statement is true?

   A The United States will be more culturally diverse.
   B Whites no longer will be the majority population.
   C The United States will be less culturally diverse.
   D The U.S. population will be larger.

PRACTICE

World History Sample

Directions: Use the pie graphs and your knowledge of world history to answer the questions below.

Government Expenditures 1992

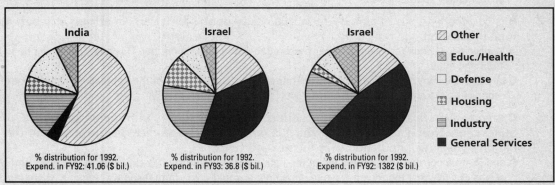

Source: Marlita Reddy, Ed., *Statistical Abstract of the World*

1 The amount of its budget that the United States spends on education and health is roughly

A one-fifth.

B one-fourth.

C one-third.

D one-half.

2 India doubles the United States in the percentage of its budget spent on

A defense.

B education and health.

C industry.

D other.

3 One possible reason that defense spending makes up such a large percentage of Israel's budget is

A Israel's history of conflict with its Arab neighbors.

B Israel's history of conflict with China.

C Israel's history of conflict with Russia.

D Israel's numerous overseas colonies.

4 Which of the following statements is true according to the graphs?

A Israel spends the most money on defense.

B The funding of education and health is the number one priority of each country.

C Every country devotes about the same percentage of its budget to "other" expenditures.

D No country devotes more than 10 percent of its budget to housing.

ANSWERS

Thinking Through the Answers

Questions from Page 34:

1 **D** is correct. Hispanic Americans more than doubled their percentage of the population, from 10.2 to 24.5 percent.
A is incorrect. Whites showed a *decrease* in their percentage of the population.
B and **C** are incorrect. While both groups increased their percentage of the population between 1995 and 2050, neither one doubled it.

2 **B** is correct. By 2050 Hispanic Americans nearly doubled African Americans as a part of the total population.
A is incorrect. Whites represent a larger percentage of the population than Hispanic Americans do in both 1995 and 2050.
C and **D** are incorrect. Hispanic Americans represent a larger portion of the population than do both these groups in 1995 and 2050.

3 **C** is correct. In the latter part of the 20th century, the majority of immigrants to the United States came from Latin America, which is reflected in the predicted large growth of the nation's Hispanic population over the next 50 years.
A and **B** are incorrect. The percentage of the nation's white population is expected to decrease, and thus it seems unlikely that the recent wave of immigration would come from these two regions where most of the residents are white.
D is incorrect. Americans of Middle Eastern descent are not shown on the graphs.

4 **A** is correct. The nation will become more diverse because each of the nation's non-white ethnic groups will account for a greater percentage of the population.
B is incorrect. Whites will still account for more than half of the nation's population, making them the majority.
C is incorrect. With the percentage of non-whites expected to increase, the nation will become more, not less, diverse.
D is incorrect. The graphs make no mention of the total population.

Questions from Page 35:

1 **D** is correct. The United States spends about 48 percent of its budget on education and health, which is equivalent to about one-half.
A, B, and **C** are incorrect.

2 **C** is correct. India spends 12.2 percent of its budget on industry, exactly double the percentage that the United States spends.
A and **B** are incorrect. The United States devotes a greater portion of its budget to these two categories than does India.
D is incorrect. The percentage of its budget that India devotes to "other" is much more than double the amount the United States spends on this category.

3 **A** is correct. Israel and its Arab neighbors share a tense relationship that has involved years of declared and undeclared warfare.
B and **C** are incorrect. Israel is engaged in no outward hostility with either of these countries.
D is incorrect. Israel does not have overseas colonies.

4 This pie graph focuses on the relationships among parts of a whole and does not examine total dollar amounts.
D is correct. No country spends more than 10 percent of its budget on housing.
A is incorrect. It is impossible to tell whether Israel spends a greater amount of money on defense than India or the United States.
B is incorrect. India does not make education and health a priority, spending only 4 percent of its budget on this category.
C is incorrect. The graph shows the United States devoting only 15.2 percent of its budget on these expenditures, and India spending 56.4 percent.

Physical Maps

Physical maps show the landforms and bodies of water in a specific area. They use color, shading, or contour lines to indicate elevation or altitude, which is also called relief. Many maps combine features of both physical and political maps—that is, they show physical characteristics as well as political boundaries.

1 Read the title to determine the area shown on the map.

2 Study the legend to find the meaning of the shadings used on the map. Typically, different shadings are used to indicate levels of elevation. Match the legend shadings to places on the map.

3 Review the labels on the map to see what physical features are shown.

4 Look at the lines of latitude and longitude. You can use this grid to identify the location of physical features.

5 Use the compass rose to determine directions on the map.

6 Use the scale to measure the actual distances between places shown on the map.

7 Read the questions and then carefully study the map to determine the answers.

World Geography Sample

1 New Zealand: Physical

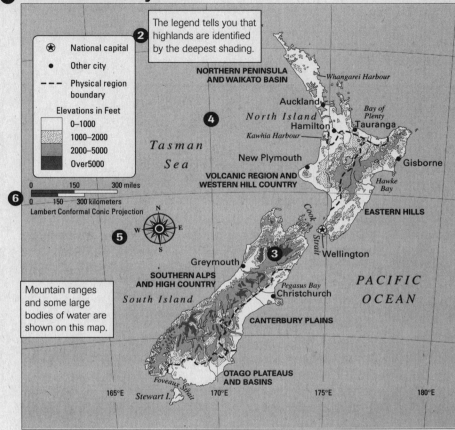

2 The legend tells you that highlands are identified by the deepest shading.

6 Mountain ranges and some large bodies of water are shown on this map.

1 South Island contains mostly

A mountains.

B plateaus.

C lowlands.

D deserts.

2 Where is the Bay of Plenty located?

A near Christchurch

B off the western coast of South Island

C off the northern coast of North Island

D near the Southern Alps and High County

answers: 1 (A), 2 (C)

Name _____   Date _____

World History and World Geography Sample

Directions: Use the map and your knowledge of world history and geography to answer the questions below.

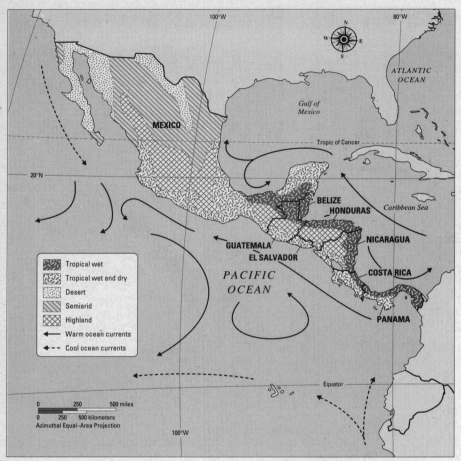

1 The country with the most uniform climate is

A Belize.

B Mexico.

C Guatemala.

D Costa Rica.

2 Based on the effect of ocean currents, temperatures in Central America most likely are in general

A cooler than in the United States.

B cooler than in South America.

C warmer than in the United States.

D the same as in the United States and South America.

3 A person might expect to encounter a rain forest in all of the following places *except*

A northern Panama.

B northern Guatemala.

C northern Mexico.

D eastern Nicaragua.

4 The ancient civilization that thrived in modern-day Mexico's tropical wet region was the

A Inca.

B Olmec.

C Anasazi.

D Hohokam.

Name _____   Date _____

World History and World Geography Sample

Directions: Use the map and your knowledge of world geography to answer the questions below.

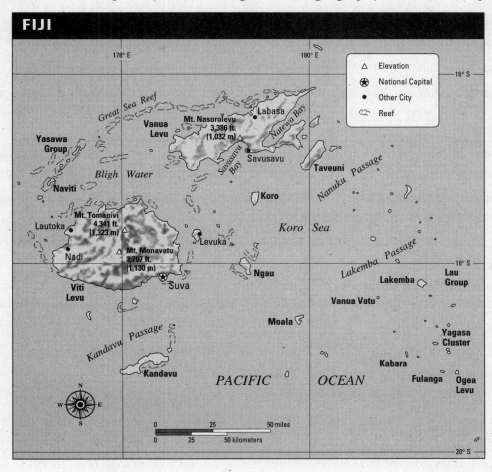

1 The city closest to Fiji's highest mountain is

A Suva.

B Labasa.

C Lautoka.

D Levuka.

2 Navigating Fiji's reefs would be of most concern to ships trying to reach the country from the

A north.

B south.

C east.

D west.

3 A traveler leaving Suva would have the shortest trip to

A Sydney.

B Santiago.

C Los Angeles.

D Reykjavik.

4 Which of the following conclusions can you draw from the map?

A Fiji is sparsely populated.

B Fiji is mostly flat.

C Little fishing goes on in Fiji.

D Parts of Fiji have a mountainous terrain.

ANSWERS

Thinking Through the Answers

Questions from Page 38:

1 **A** is correct. Belize has one dominant climate—tropical wet.

   B, C, and **D** are incorrect. Mexico has five climate patterns, Guatemala has three, and Costa Rica has two.

2 Recall that ocean currents influence a region's climate.

   C is correct. Central America is home to warmer climates than those in the United States or South America.
   A, B, and **D** are incorrect. Climates in Central America are warmer than in the United States and South America.

3 You should determine that rain forests are found in a climate that is tropical wet. Then look for an answer that includes a region where rain forests would most likely **not** exist.

   C is correct. Northern Mexico has desert and semiarid climate, thus is an unlikely place for a rain forest.
   A, B, and **D** are incorrect. All have tropical wet climates.

4 **B** is correct. The Olmec created a civilization out of the wet and swampy region of present-day southern Mexico.

   A is incorrect. The Inca built their empire along the Andes Mountains in South America.
   C and **D** are incorrect. The Anasazi and Hohokam emerged in what is today the southwestern United States.

Questions from Page 39:

1 First, you must determine that Fiji's highest mountain is Mt. Tomanivi.

   C is correct. Of all the cities listed, Lautoka sits closest to Mt. Tomanivi.
   A, B, and **D** are incorrect. These cities are not close to Mt. Tomanivi.

2 **A** is correct. As the map indicates, reefs form a near complete line along the waters to the north of Fiji.

   B , C, and **D** are incorrect. There are relatively few reefs to the east, west, or south of the country.

3 Recall that Fiji is located in the South Pacific near Australia.

   A is correct. Sydney is the capital of Australia.
   B, C, and **D** are incorrect. Los Angeles is located in the United States, Santiago is located in South America, and Reykjavik is the capital of Iceland. All countries are farther from Fiji than Australia is.

4 **D** is correct. The presence of several significant mountains indicates that parts of Fiji have mountainous terrain.

   A is incorrect. Neither the map nor the legend provides any population information.
   B and **C** are incorrect. The presence of mountains demonstrates that Fiji is not mostly flat and its location in the Pacific Ocean suggests that fishing probably takes place.

Thematic Maps

A thematic map, or special-purpose map, focuses on a particular topic. Population density, election results, migration routes, a country's economic activities, international alliances, and major battles in a war are all topics you might see illustrated on a thematic map.

1 Thematic maps show specialized information. Read the title to discover the subject and purpose of the map.

2 Study the labels on the map to find more information about its subject and purpose.

3 Examine the legend to find the meaning of any symbols and shadings used on the map.

4 Locate the symbols and shadings on the map and try to make generalizations or draw conclusions about the information they convey.

5 Read the questions and carefully study the map to determine the answers.

United States History Sample

1 **Texas Railroads in the Late 1880s**

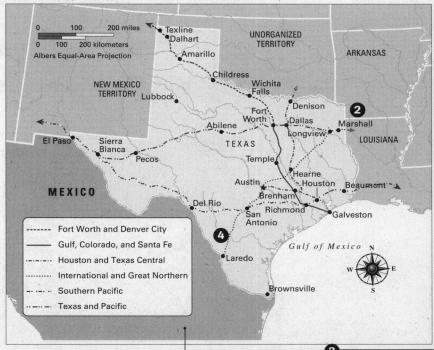

3 While a thematic map focuses on one topic, it often offers several kinds of information on that topic. So, the legend for a thematic map often is quite detailed.

5 **1** In which Texas city did the Gulf, Colorado, and Santa Fe railroad begin?

A Beaumont

B Del Rio

C El Paso

D Galveston

2 If you traveled from Amarillo to Abilene by way of Fort Worth, which railroad would you board in Fort Worth to complete your journey?

A Fort Worth and Denver City

B International and Great Northern

C Southern Pacific

D Texas and Pacific

answers: 1 (D), 2 (D)

Name _____ Date _____

World History Sample

Directions: Use the map and your knowledge of world history to answer the questions below.

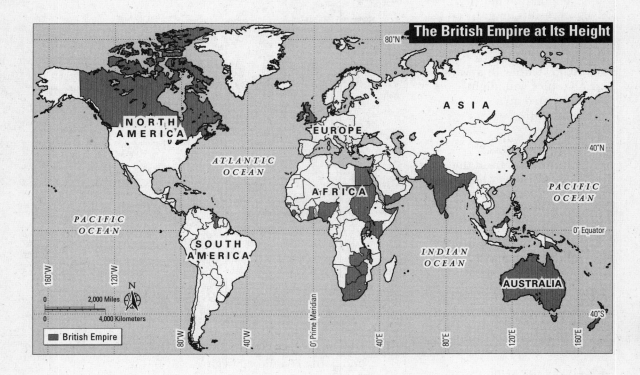

1 Britain most likely had to devote the most effort to colonial rule on the continent of

  A Asia.
  B Europe.
  C Africa.
  D South America.

2 Ships moving raw materials from Canada to Great Britain would travel

  A east.
  B west.
  C north.
  D south.

3 The country known as the "jewel" of the British empire and the main producer of the highly profitable commodity tea was

  A Egypt.
  B India.
  C Australia.
  D South Africa.

4 Based on the map, you could conclude that Great Britain had

  A low unemployment.
  B large cities.
  C a powerful military.
  D an unfavorable balance of trade.

Name _____ Date _____

PRACTICE

World Geography Sample

Directions: Use the map and your knowledge of world geography to answer the questions below.

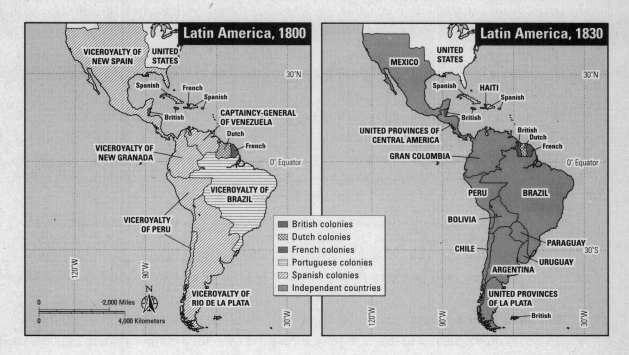

1 The independence movements in Latin America between 1800 and 1830 had the greatest impact on

   A Britain.
   B Spain.
   C Portugal.
   D France.

2 Between 1800 and 1830, Great Britain

   A remained in control of Cuba.
   B seized Brazil from the Portuguese.
   C lost the most colonies in Latin America.
   D gained colonies in Latin America.

3 Which independent nations emerged from the Vice Royalty of New Spain?

   A the United Provinces of Central America and Mexico
   B the United States, Mexico, and the United Provinces of Central America
   C Gran Colombia and the United Provinces of Central America
   D Peru, Bolivia, and Chile

4 Which of the following statements is true according to the map?

   A Much of the Caribbean remained under European control.
   B Portugal maintained a colonial presence in Latin America.
   C Argentina became the largest country in South America.
   D During this period, the United States decreased in size.

ANSWERS

Thinking Through the Answers

Questions from Page 42:

1 **C** is correct. Of all the continents listed, Africa is the one with the most British colonies and thus would seem to be the one that required the most effort at colonial rule.

2 **A** is correct. To answer this question, you must be able to locate both Great Britain and Canada. Canada lies directly west of Great Britain, and thus any materials flowing to the mother country would travel east.

3 **A** is incorrect. You should recall that India was "jewel" of the British empire and its main supplier of tea.

4 **C** is correct. Because Great Britain had so many colonies on many continents, one can conclude that the nation needed a large and powerful military to maintain order in such a far-flung empire.

   A and **B** are incorrect. It is impossible to tell from this particular map whether either of these was a characteristic of Great Britain.

   D is incorrect. With such a large empire giving it access to so many resources, Britain probably did not have to purchase many materials from other countries. As a result, it most likely enjoyed a favorable balance of trade.

Questions from Page 43:

1 **B** is correct. Spain had the most colonies in Latin America and thus was impacted the most by the independence movements in the region.

2 **D** is correct. Britain is the only nation to actually gain colonies during this time period, as it occupied new lands without losing its old territories.

   A is incorrect. By knowing the location of Cuba (just off the tip of Florida), you can see that the island remained in Spanish hands between 1800 and 1830.

   B is incorrect. Brazil did not fall to the British but gained its independence.

   C is incorrect. As the map shows, Spain was the nation with the greatest presence in Latin America and thus was the country that lost the most colonies.

3 **B** is correct. The Viceroyalty of New Spain contained parts of all three nations listed.

   A is incorrect. It does not include the United States.

   C is incorrect. The nations listed were part of the Viceroyalty of New Granada.

   D is incorrect. The nations listed were part of the Viceroyalty of Peru.

4 **A** is correct. The Caribbean is made up of the cluster of islands between the United States and South America. As the map indicates, most of these islands remained in European hands.

   B is incorrect. By 1830, Portugal had no colonies in Latin America.

   C is incorrect. Brazil is the largest country in South America.

   D is incorrect. The United States increased in size during this period.

Time Lines

A time line is a type of chart that lists historical events in the order in which they occurred. In other words, time lines are a visual method of showing what happened when.

1 Read the title to discover the subject of the time line.

2 Identify the period of history covered in the time line by noting the first and last dates shown.

3 Read the events in chronological order. Notice the intervals between events.

4 Note how events are related to one another. Look particularly for cause-effect relationships.

5 Make generalizations about the information presented in the time line.

6 Use the information you have gathered from the above strategies to answer the questions.

United States History Sample

1 The Civil Rights Movement, 1940s–1960s

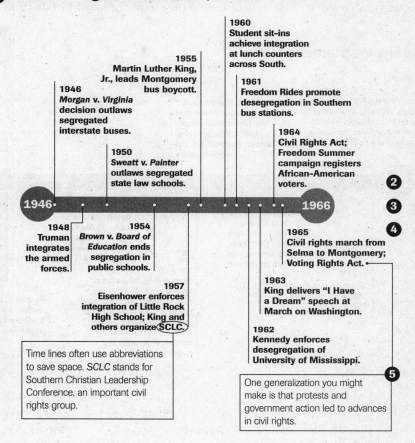

1946
Morgan v. *Virginia* decision outlaws segregated interstate buses.

1950
Sweatt v. *Painter* outlaws segregated state law schools.

1955
Martin Luther King, Jr., leads Montgomery bus boycott.

1960
Student sit-ins achieve integration at lunch counters across South.

1961
Freedom Rides promote desegregation in Southern bus stations.

1964
Civil Rights Act; Freedom Summer campaign registers African-American voters.

1948
Truman integrates the armed forces.

1954
Brown v. *Board of Education* ends segregation in public schools.

1957
Eisenhower enforces integration of Little Rock High School; King and others organize SCLC.

1965
Civil rights march from Selma to Montgomery; Voting Rights Act.

1963
King delivers "I Have a Dream" speech at March on Washington.

1962
Kennedy enforces desegregation of University of Mississippi.

Time lines often use abbreviations to save space. *SCLC* stands for Southern Christian Leadership Conference, an important civil rights group.

One generalization you might make is that protests and government action led to advances in civil rights.

1 Which was the first major civil rights activity in which Martin Luther King, Jr., was involved?

A "I Have a Dream" speech

B march from Selma to Montgomery

C Montgomery bus boycott

D organization of the SCLC

2 The success of the civil rights movement resulted from organized protests by African Americans and actions by

A state courts.

B reformed state governments.

C federal courts and Congress.

D all three branches of the federal government.

Recall that southern state governments often resisted civil rights in this period. Therefore, you can eliminate alternatives **F** and **G**.

answers: 1(C), 2(D)

PRACTICE

World History Sample

Directions: Use the time line and your knowledge of world history to answer the questions below.

Modern Vietnamese History

1946
War erupts as France invades Vietnam in an effort to reclaim control over its former colony; United States provides aid to French war effort.

1956
South Vietnam boycott selections for fear that the Communist North would win; U.S. provides financial and military aid to the South.

1973
Peace agreement ends the war; last U.S. forces leave Vietnam.

1940   **1980**

1945
Japan surrenders to the Allies and leaves Vietnam; nationalist leader Ho Chi Minh declares Vietnam an independent nation.

1957
Communist rebels in the South, known as the Vietcong, begin a guerilla war against the government.

1968
Vietcong launch Tet Offensive, a multi-city attack that prompts many Americans to doubt the war effort.

1975
North Vietnam conquers South Vietnam and unifies the country under Communist rule.

1941
Japan seizes Vietnam from French during World War II.

1954
France withdraws from Vietnam after suffering a major defeat at the battle of Dien Bien Phu; Geneva Accords divide Vietnam into two and call for elections to unify the country in 1956.

1965
First U.S. troops arrive in South Vietnam to help battle the Vietcong.

1 The foreign nation that spent the longest time in Vietnam during these years was

A France.

B Japan.

C the Vietcong.

D the United States.

2 The years 1954 and 1968 have in common

A significant military setbacks for the Vietnamese.

B significant military victories for the Vietnamese.

C significant military setbacks for the French.

D significant military setbacks for the Americans.

3 The Vietcong were allies of which fighting force?

A South Vietnamese

B North Vietnamese

C the United States

D Vietnamese nationalists

4 Based on the time line, you can make the generalization that the modern history of Vietnam was one of

A steady economic growth.

B poor agricultural production.

C near constant warfare.

D relative peace.

PRACTICE

World Geography Sample

Directions: Use the time line and your knowledge of world geography to answer the questions below.

The Age of Exploration

1498
Portuguese explorer
Vasco de Gama rounds
and reaches India.

1500
Portuguese explorer
Pedro Álvares Cabral
reaches modern-day
Brazil.

1492
Sailor Christopher
Columbus claims the
Caribbean islands for Spain.

1607
English settle colony of
Jamestown on the shores
of modern-day Virginia.

1400 — **1610**

1405
Chinese explorer Zheng
He began the first of his
voyages throughout
Southeast Asia.

1488
Portuguese sailor
Bartolomeu Dias
rounds the southern
tip of Africa.

1519
Portuguese explorer
Ferdinand Magellan
embarks on round-
the-world voyage.

1533
Spanish explorer Francisco
Pizarro conquers the Inca
empire in South America.

1534
Frenchman Jacques Cartier
explores the present-day
St. Lawrence River.

1 How long after the Spanish began settling the Americas did England establish its first permanent colony in the region?

A 74 years
B 86 years
C 115 years
D 202 years

2 One could conclude from the time line that the most dominant colonial power in the Americas early on would be

A England.
B Spain.
C France.
D Portugal.

3 All of the following participated in the exploration of the so-called "new world" *except*

A Hernando Cortés.
B Francisco Pizarro.
C Vasco da Gama.
D Christopher Columbus.

4 Based on the exploration of Jacques Cartier, you can infer that the colony of New France would be located in

A Africa.
B Asia.
C South America.
D North America.

ANSWERS

Thinking Through the Answers

Questions from Page 46:

1 **D** is correct. According to the time line, the United States spent from 1965 to 1973 in Vietnam, longer than any other nation depicted on the time line. Thus **A** and **B** are incorrect.

C is incorrect. The Vietcong, as the time line states, were a group of Vietnamese Communist rebels, not a foreign country.

2 **B** is correct. As the time line shows, the Vietnamese scored major military victories, not setbacks, during these years. Thus **A** is incorrect.

C is incorrect. The French were out of Vietnam by 1968 and thus were not involved in any military action there that year.

D is incorrect. The Americans had not yet entered Vietnam in 1954 and thus were not involved in any military action there that year.

3 **B** is correct. The Vietcong fought against South Vietnamese forces and their allies, the United States.

A and **C** are incorrect. Both forces fought against the Vietcong.

D is incorrect. There were no forces identified as Vietnamese nationalists.

4 **C** is correct. The description of one conflict after another on the time line makes this the correct answer. Thus **D** is incorrect.

A and **B** are incorrect. It is impossible to tell from the time line whether Vietnam experienced either economic growth or a decline in agricultural production during these years.

Questions from Page 47:

1 **C** is correct. This answer marks the number of years between Spain's initial settlement of the Americas by Columbus and the establishment of Jamestown.

A, B, and **D** are incorrect. None of the other answers uses these two dates.

2 **B** is correct. Spain has the most entries with regard to exploration and conquest of the Americas and thus seems to be the country that would dominate the region.

A, C, and **D** are incorrect. Each of these countries had just one entry on the time line with regard to exploration of the Americas.

3 To answer this question correctly, you need to recall that the "new world" referred to the Americas, lands that had been unknown to Europeans.

C is correct. Da Gama sailed east to Asia, not west to the Americas.
A, B, and **D** are incorrect. Cortés, Pizarro, and Columbus explored the lands of the "new world."

4 To answer this question correctly, you need to recall that the St. Lawrence River is located in Canada.

D is correct. Canada is located in North America.

Constructed Response

Constructed-response questions focus on various kinds of documents. Each document is accompanied by one or more short-answer questions. For the most part, the answers to these questions can be found directly in the document. Some answers, however, require knowledge of the subject or time period addressed in the document.

① Read the title of the document to discover the subject addressed in the questions.

② Carefully study the document and take notes on what you see.

③ Read the questions and then study the document again to locate the answers.

④ Carefully write your answers. Unless the directions say otherwise, your answers need not be complete sentences.

World Geography Sample

① **Japanese–American Interment**

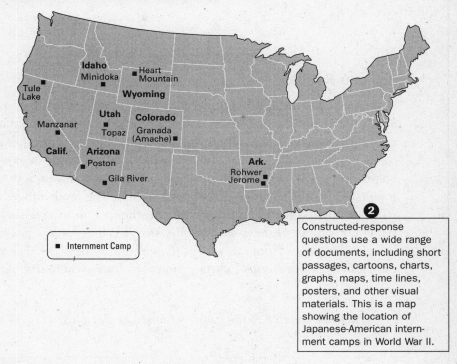

■ Internment Camp

② Constructed-response questions use a wide range of documents, including short passages, cartoons, charts, graphs, maps, time lines, posters, and other visual materials. This is a map showing the location of Japanese-American internment camps in World War II.

③ **1** Which states had more than one relocation camp?

④ _Arkansas, Arizona, California_

2 In which region of the country were most relocation camps located?

Southwest

3 What event led to calls for Japanese Americans to be removed from the Pacific Coast?

the Japanese attack on Pearl Harbor

PRACTICE

World History Sample

Directions: Use the following passage and your knowledge of world history to answer the questions below.

The Incan Roads

The Inca, a civilization that flourished along the Andes Mountains in South America from about 100 to 1535, were extraordinary organizers and administrators. To control the huge empire, the rulers divided their territory and its people into manageable units, governed by a central bureaucracy. They also constructed an elaborate system of roads. A marvel of engineering, this 14,000-mile-long network of roads and bridges spanned the empire, traversing rugged mountains and harsh desert. The roads ranged from paved stone to simple paths. Along the roads, the Inca built guesthouses to provide shelter for weary travelers. A system of runners, known as *chasquis,* traveled these roads as a kind of postal service, carrying messages from one end of the empire to the other. The road system also allowed the easy movement of troops to bring control to zones where trouble might be brewing.

1 What was the role of the runners known as *chasquis?*

_____

_____

2 How did the road system help the Inca to maintain control over their large empire?

_____

_____

3 How did the Inca's elaborate road network play a role in the empire's collapse?

_____

_____

_____

PRACTICE

United States History Sample

Directions: Use the information in the chart to create a bar graph showing the differences between men and women in yearly earnings in the following categories: Accountant, Cook, Teacher, Physician, Nurse, Retail Sales Worker

Women's and Men's Average Yearly Earnings in Selected Careers, 1982

Career	Women	Men
Accountant	$19,916	$25,272
Advertising Manager	19,396	32,292
Computer Operator	13,728	17,992
Cook	8,476	9,880
Engineer	26,052	31,460
Financial Manager	19,136	30,004
High School Teacher	18,980	21,424
Insurance Salesperson	15,236	22,152
Lawyer	30,264	34,008
Personnel Specialist	17,836	26,832
Physician	21,944	26,884
Police/Detective	15,548	20,072
Real Estate Salesperson	16,432	24,076
Registered Nurse	20,592	20,696
Retail Sales Worker	8,736	13,728
Social Worker	15,600	20,436
University Professor	20,748	26,832

1 Which of the careers probably do *not* require a college education?

_____

2 How do the salaries of college-degreed persons compare with those not having a college education?

_____

ANSWERS

Thinking Through the Answers

Questions from Page 50:

1   to deliver messages from one end of the empire to the other

2   It facilitated communication and troop movement across the empire.

3   It enabled Spanish forces led by Francisco Pizarro to easily march through the empire.

Questions from Page 51:

1   cook, insurance salesperson, real estate salesperson, retail sales worker

2   Most of the degreed persons make more than those without a college degree. Some of the lowest paid degreed persons make about double that of those without a college degree.

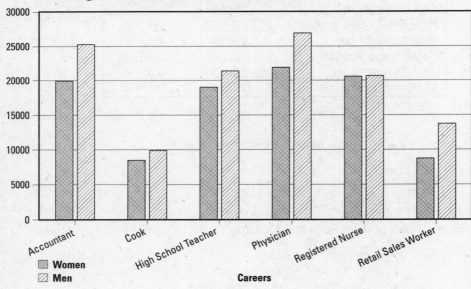

Women's and Men's Average Yearly Earnings in Selected Careers, 1982

Extended Response

Extended-response questions, like constructed-response questions, usually focus on one type of document. However, they are more complex and require more time to complete than typical short-answer constructed-response questions. Some extended-response questions ask you to present information from the document in a different form. Others ask you to write an essay or report or some other extended piece of writing. Sometimes you are required to apply your knowledge of geography or history to information contained in the document.

❶ Read the title of the document to get an idea of the subject.

❷ Study and analyze the document.

❸ Carefully read each extended-response question.

❹ If the question calls for a drawing, such as a diagram, graph, or chart, make a rough sketch on scrap paper first. Then make a final copy of your drawing on the answer sheet.

❺ If the question requires an essay, jot down your ideas in outline form. Use this outline to write your answer.

World Geography Sample

❶ ### Causes of Death in Developed and Developing Countries, 1993

❷

Cause	Developed countries (percentage of deaths)	Developing countries (percentage of deaths)
Infections and parasites	1.2	41.5
Respiratory diseases	7.8	5.0
Cancers	21.6	8.9
Circulatory diseases	46.7	10.7
Childbirth	0	1.3
Infant mortality	0.7	7.9
Injury	7.5	7.9
Other causes	14.5	16.8

Source: "Causes of Death, 1993," from *Oxford Atlas of World History,* edited by Patrick K. O'Brien. Copyright © 1999 by Oxford University Press. All rights reserved. Reprinted by permission of Oxford University Press.

❸ **1** Use the information in the chart to create a bar graph showing the causes of death in developed and developing countries.

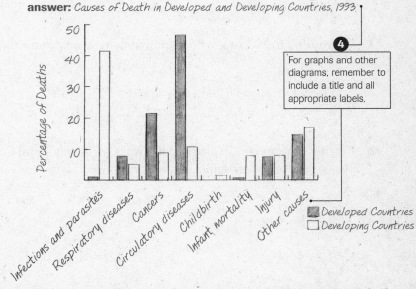

answer: *Causes of Death in Developed and Developing Countries, 1993*

❹ For graphs and other diagrams, remember to include a title and all appropriate labels.

❸ **2** Write a short essay summarizing what the chart and graph show about the major causes of death in developed and developing countries. Give a possible explanation for the data.

❺

Outline

I. Major causes of death
  A. Infections and parasites-poor
  B. Circulatory diseases-developed

II. Explanations
  A. Poor sanitation and health care
  B. Rich diet, no exercise, smoking

PRACTICE

United States History Sample

Directions: Use the document and your knowledge of U.S. history to answer the items below.

Confronting McCarthyism

This is no time for men who oppose Senator McCarthy's methods to keep silent, or for those who approve. We can deny our heritage and our history, but we cannot escape responsibility for the result. As a nation we have come into our full inheritance at a tender age. We proclaim ourselves, as indeed we are, the defenders of freedom—what's left of it—but we cannot defend freedom abroad by deserting it at home. The actions of the junior senator from Wisconsin have caused alarm and dismay amongst our allies abroad and given considerable comfort to our enemies. And whose fault is that? Not really his; he didn't create the situation of fear, he merely exploited it and rather successfully. Cassius was right: "The fault, dear Brutus, is not in our stars but in ourselves."

—Edward R. Murrow

Excerpted from "TV Comment on Joseph McCarthy, 1954" by Edward R. Murrow, from *In Search of Light: The Broadcasts of Edward R. Murrow, 1938–1961,* edited by Edward Bliss, Jr.

1   According to Murrow, who is ultimately responsible for the rise of McCarthyism?

    _____

    _____

2   Write a short essay explaining the ways McCarthy's anti-Communist crusade undermined the values of American democracy.

PRACTICE

World History Sample

Directions: Use the document and your knowledge of world history to answer the items below.

The Treaty of Versailles

The Treaty of Versailles: Major Provisions			
League of Nations	**Territorial Losses**	**Military Restrictions**	**War Guilt**
• International peace organization; membership to include Allied war powers and 32 Allied and neutral nations • Germany and Russia excluded	• Germany returns Alsace-Lorraine to France; French border extended to the west bank of the Rhine River • Germany surrenders all of its overseas colonies in Africa and the Pacific	• Limits set on the size of the German army • Germany prohibited from importing or manufacturing weapons or war materiel • Germany forbidden to build or buy submarines or have an air force	• Sole responsibility for the war placed on Germany's shoulders • Germany forced to pay the Allies $33 billion in reparations over 30 years

1   How might the average German have reacted to the treaty? Write a short essay supporting your opinion.

2   Write a short essay in which you explain how the Treaty of Versailles created what many considered a flawed peace.

ANSWERS

Thinking Through the Answers

Below you will find the answers to the questions on the Practice pages. Study the explanations to clarify your thinking on how to answer the questions.

Questions from Page 54:

1 The citizens of the United States were responsible for creating the atmosphere of fear and panic about communism that allowed someone like Joseph McCarthy to rise to prominence.

2 **ANSWER RUBRIC** The best answers will point out that McCarthy accused people of allegiance to communism without providing proof of such charges. This is contrary to the very foundation on which America's legal system is built—that people accused of crimes or wrongdoing are presented with the evidence against them. McCarthy's crusade also left many people afraid to say anything that might be viewed as traitorous or disloyal. Thus, Americans felt like they no longer possessed freedom of speech, one of the nation's most cherished rights and one guaranteed by the First Amendment of the U.S. Constitution.

Questions from Page 55:

1 **ANSWER RUBRIC** The best answers will point out that most Germans probably reacted angrily to the treaty because it singled out Germany for such harsh punishment. Germans most likely resented the fact that their country was forced to relinquish territories and endure various military restrictions. More significantly, the German people probably felt that the treaty, especially the war-guilt clause, unfairly blamed Germany alone for a war that they felt erupted out of Europe's complex alliance system and involved numerous countries.

2 **ANSWER RUBRIC** The best answers will point out that by so harshly punishing Germany, the treaty fostered great anger and resentment among the German people. In the years to come, Adolf Hitler and the Nazi Party would capitalize on this lingering resentment to seize power in Germany. The treaty also ignored Russia's contribution to the war effort, excluding the Russians from the peace conference and disregarding their lost territory. In the wake of the war, Russia became determined to regain its former lands. In addition, the treaty ignored the independence claims of many colonized peoples, which angered numerous ethnic groups and only heightened international instability. Furthermore, the League of Nations turned out to be a largely powerless body that did little to halt acts of aggression during the 1920s and 1930s. In the eyes of many observers, the shortcomings of the treaty helped to pave the way for World War II.

Document-Based Question

A document-based question (DBQ) requires you to analyze and interpret a variety of documents. These documents often are accompanied by short-answer questions. You use these answers and information from the documents to write an essay on a specified subject.

1 Read the "Historical Context" section to get a sense of the issue addressed in the question.

2 Read the "Task" section and note the action words. This will help you understand exactly what the essay question requires.

3 Study and analyze each document. Consider what connection the documents have to the essay question. Take notes on your ideas.

4 Read and answer the document-specific questions. Think about how these questions connect to the essay topic.

World History Sample

Introduction

1 **Historical Context:** For hundreds of years, Mongol nomads lived in separate tribes, sometimes fighting among themselves. In the early 1200s, a new leader—Genghis Khan—united these tribes and turned the Mongols into a powerful fighting force.

2 **Task:** Discuss how the Mongols achieved their conquest of Central and East Asia and what impact their rule had on Europeans.

Part 1: Short Answer

Study each document carefully and answer the questions that follow.

3 Document 1: Mongol Warrior

4 **What were the characteristics of Mongol warriors?**

The Mongol soldiers were excellent horsemen who could travel great distances without rest. They attacked swiftly and without mercy, they used clever psychological warfare to strike fear into their enemies, and they adopted new weapons and technology.

⑤ Carefully read the essay question. Then write an outline for your essay.

⑥ Write your essay. Be sure that it has an introductory paragraph that introduces your argument, main body paragraphs that explain it, and a concluding paragraph that restates your position. In your essay, include quotations or details from specific documents to support your ideas. Add other supporting facts or details that you know from your study of world history.

Document 2: The Mongol Empire

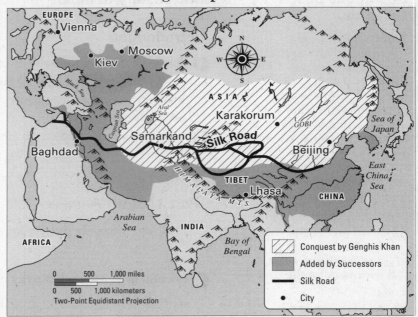

What route connected the Mongol Empire to Europe? What was the major purpose of this route?

The Silk Road; it was the major trade route between Asia and Europe.

Document 3: The Great Khan's Wealth

Let me tell you further that several times a year a [command] goes forth through the towns that all those who have gems and pearls and gold and silver must bring them to the Great Khan's mint. This they do, and in such abundance that it is past all reckoning; and they are all paid in paper money. By this means the Great Khan acquires all the gold and silver and pearls and precious stones of all his territories.

—Marco Polo, *The Travels of Marco Polo* (c. 1300)

How did Marco Polo's descriptions of his travels encourage European interest in East Asia?

Europeans were attracted by his descriptions of the great wealth.

⑤ Part 2: Essay

Using information from the documents, your answers to the questions in Part 1, and your knowledge of world history, write an essay discussing how the Mongols conquered Central and East Asia and what affects their rule had on Europeans. ⑥

PRACTICE

United States History Sample

Directions: Use your knowledge of United States history to answer the questions below.

Introduction

Historical Context: During the late 1800s, the United States underwent a great transformation, as the growth of industrialization and increased immigration led to rapid urbanization. While cities provided new opportunities for millions of Americans, they also created problems and challenges.

Task: Discuss the reasons for the rapid growth of cities in the late 1800s and describe the effects of urban growth on American society.

Part 1: Short Answer

Study each document carefully and answer the questions that follow.

Document 1: European Emigration, 1820–1920

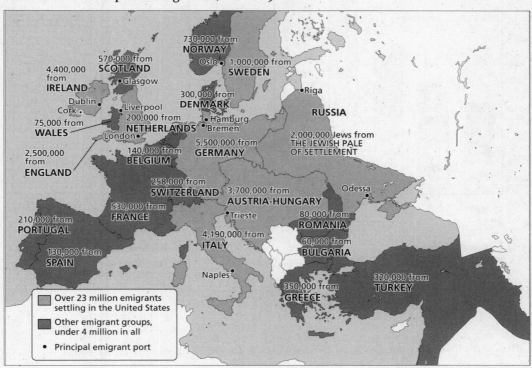

1   Which three countries sent the greatest number of immigrants to the United States?

_____

2   In which region of Europe are the greatest number of emigrant ports?

_____

Document-Based Question written by Patricia Zalewski,
Liverpool High School, Liverpool, New York

PRACTICE

Document 2: U.S. Farm and Nonfarm Workers, 1860–1900 and Average Annual Income for Farm and Nonfarm Workers, 1860–1900

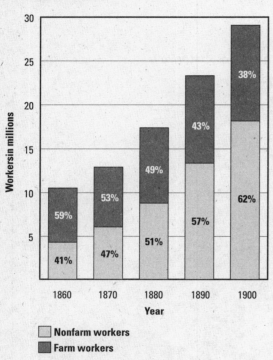

U.S. Farm and Nonfarm Workers, 1860-1990

Nonfarm workers
Farm workers

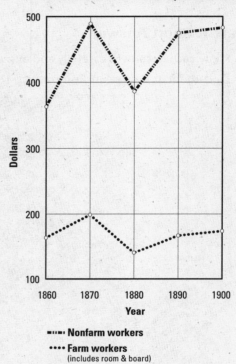

Average Annual Income for Farm and NonFarm Workers, 1860-1900

Nonfarm workers
Farm workers
(includes room & board)

Source: *Historical Statistics of the United States: Colonial Times to 1970*

1   Roughly how many more nonfarm workers were there in 1900 than in 1860?

_____

2   How did annual farm income compare to annual nonfarm income during this period?

_____

PRACTICE

Document 3: From Jacob Riis's *How the Other Half Lives*

Be a little careful, please! The hall is dark and you might stumble over the children pitching pennies back there. Not that it would hurt them; kicks and cuffs are their daily diet. They have little else. . . . Close [stuffy]? Yes! What would you have? All the fresh air that ever enters these stairs comes from the hall-door that is forever slamming. . . . Here is a door. Listen! That short hacking cough, that tiny, helpless wail—what do they mean? . . . The child is dying with measles. With half a chance it might have lived; but it had none. That dark bedroom killed it.

—Jacob Riis, *How the Other Half Lives*

Name two difficulties of urban life described in Jacob Riis's passage or revealed in the photo.

_____

_____

_____

PRACTICE

Document 4: From Jack London's "The Story of an Eye-witness"

On Wednesday morning at a quarter past five came the earthquake. A minute later the flames were leaping upward. In a dozen different quarters south of Market Street, in the working-class ghetto, and in the factories, fires started. There was no opposing the flames. . . . And the great water-mains had burst. All the shrewd contrivances and safeguards of man had been thrown out of gear by thirty seconds' twitching of the earth-crust.

Fire: Enemy of the City

The Great Chicago Fire October 8–10, 1871	**The San Francisco Earthquake** April 18, 1906
· The fire burned for 29 hours.	· The quake lasted 28 seconds; fires burned for 4 days.
· An estimated 300 people died.	· An estimated 1,000 people died.
· 100,000 were left homeless.	· 250,000 were left homeless.
· More than 3 square miles of the city center was destroyed.	· Fire swept through 5 square miles of the city.
· Property loss was estimated at $200 million.	· Property loss was estimated at $500 million.
· 17,500 buildings were destroyed.	· 28,000 buildings were destroyed.

How do the passage and infographic illustrate the dangers of a natural disaster in an urban area?

_____

_____

_____

_____

PRACTICE

Document 5: From Jane Addams's *Twenty Years at Hull-House*

In those early days we often were asked why we had come to live on Halsted Street when we could afford to live somewhere else. . . .

From the first it seemed understood that we were ready to perform the humblest neighborhood services. We were asked to wash the newborn babies, and to prepare the dead for burial, to nurse the sick, and to "mind the children."

Occasionally these neighborly offices unexpectedly uncovered ugly human traits. For six weeks after an operation we kept in one of our three bedrooms a forlorn little baby who, because he was born with a cleft palate, was most unwelcome even to his mother, and we were horrified when he died of neglect a week after he was returned to his home; a little Italian bride of fifteen sought shelter with us one November evening, to escape her husband who had beaten her every night for a week when he returned home from work, because she had lost her wedding ring. . . .

Perhaps even in those first days we made a beginning toward that object which was afterwards stated in our charter: "To provide a center for a higher civic and social life; to institute and maintain educational and philanthropic enterprises; and to investigate and improve conditions in the industrial districts of Chicago."

—Jane Addams, *Twenty Years at Hull-House* (Urbana: University of Illinois Press, 1990), pp. 65–66

1 What types of services did Hull House perform for the neighborhood?

_____

_____

2 According to Jane Addams, what were the goals of Hull House?

_____

_____

_____

Document 6: Origins of the Cable Car

I was largely induced to think over the matter from seeing the difficulty and pain the horses experienced in hauling the cars up Jackson Street, from Kearny to Stockton Street, on which street four or five horses were needed for the purpose—the driving being accompanied by the free use of whip and voice, and occasionally by the horses falling and being dragged down the hill on their sides, by the car loaded with passengers sliding on its track. . . . With the view of obviating [preventing] these difficulties . . . I devoted all my available time to the careful consideration of the subject.

—Andrew Smith Hallidie, inventor of the cable car, from the Museum of the City of San Francisco Web site

Why did Hallidie believe that transportation methods in the city needed improving?

_____

_____

_____

_____

_____

PRACTICE

Document 7: New Ways to Play, 1877–1917

Central Park, New York City

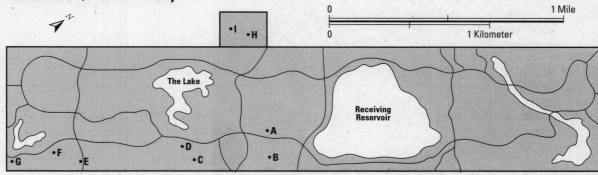

A Cleopatra's Needle
B Metropolitan Museum of Art
C Alice in Wonderland Statue
D Hans Christian Andersen Statue
E Children's Zoo
F Zoo
G General Sherman Statue
H Hayden Planetarium
I American Museum of Natural History

How did Central Park improve the lives of all classes in the city?

_____

_____

_____

_____

_____

PRACTICE

Document 8: Fifth Avenue at Madison Square, New York City

Fifth Avenue at Madison Square, 1894–1895 by Theodore Robinson. Oil on canvas 24 1/8 x 19 1/4 in. (61.3 x 48.9 cm). Gift of Ferdinand Howald, Columbus Museum of Art.

What does this painting suggest about the living conditions of some citizens of New York City?

_____

_____

_____

Part 2: Essay

Using information from the documents, your responses to the short answer questions, and your knowledge of U.S. history, write an essay that explains the causes and consequences of urbanization, as well as the effort to address the numerous challenges presented by the rapid growth of cities.

PRACTICE

Thinking Through the Answers

Part 1: Short Answer

Document 1

1   Germany–5.5 million; Ireland–4.4 million; and Italy–4.19 million

2   northwest Europe

Document 2

1   about 16 million

2   Farm income remained about the same while nonfarm income rose about $100.

Document 3

People lived in impoverished and unsanitary conditions, there was little privacy, and diseases spread easily.

Document 4

The crowded and built-up conditions of a city made earthquakes all the more destructive as they buckled streets and broke water mains, and thus made it difficult to fight the resulting fires and to rescue people.

Document 5

1   Hull House took care of babies and children, prepared the dead for burial, tended to the sick, and provided shelter to anyone who might need it.

2   to promote educational and charitable work and to provide a better quality of life for the poor of Chicago

Document 6

The system consisted mainly of horse-drawn carriages, which were difficult to drive and tended to tip over on the city's steep and crowded streets. They were dangerous to animals and humans.

Document 7

It provided an area where people could relax and escape from their daily work. It had open green space, walkways, lakes, and was free.

Document 8

Some residents of the city were wealthy and lived comfortably.

Part 2: Essay

Pre-writing Essay Checklist

- ☐ **1** Have I read the historical context and task carefully so I understand what I am supposed to be writing about?

- ☐ **2** Have I read each of the documents?

- ☐ **3** Can I establish a relationship or links between some or all of the documents?

- ☐ **4** Have I thought of a topic sentence and a basic outline for my essay?

- ☐ **5** Do I have a conclusion for my essay?

Rubrics

The best essays will link all the documents into a coherent examination of the changes in the United States as a result of rapid urbanization. First, the essay will identify the causes of urbanization, citing the information in Document 2 as support. The information in Documents 1 and 2 can be used to describe the demographic make-up of the new urban dwellers. Next, the essay should analyze the problems that resulted as an outgrowth of urbanization; evidence from Documents 3, 4, and 5 should be cited. Changes in the physical aspects of the city as evidenced in Documents 6 and 7 should also be included.

Finally, it should be noted that not everyone living in the city lived in squalor. The city also became the location of wealthy families enjoying the amenities of the city as seen in Document 8. The essay should have a logical conclusion that summarizes the points made in the body of the composition.

Post-writing Checklist

- ☐ **1** Do I have a topic sentence for my essay?

- ☐ **2** Do my points follow in logical succession?

- ☐ **3** Do I have a summary and conclusion for my essay?

- ☐ **4** Have I checked and corrected grammar, spelling, and punctuation errors in my work?

Part 3: SAT I and ACT Practice

To the Student

STRATEGIES FOR TAKING THE READING SECTIONS OF THE ACT AND SAT I

A few years ago, a number of highly successful professional people were asked to take the SAT I or the ACT, just as they had done years before in high school. They refused. They bluntly, positively, out-and-out refused. Not one of them said, "Hey, that sounds like fun! Just say when!" So, if you dread the day when you'll be sitting down, sharpened pencil in hand, to face one of these tests, you're not alone. If you're convinced that taking these tests is the worst thing you'll ever have to do, again, you're not alone. But you don't have to feel that way. And being prepared is the best way to help you feel differently.

WHY DO PEOPLE DO THIS TO YOU?

Why do you have to take these tests? Because college admissions officers think your scores will predict how well you'll do in college. Whether they really do is questionable, because the test scores do not measure how smart you are, how well-organized you are, how hard-working you are, or how interested you are in learning. Actually, your grades in high school are usually a better predictor of how well you'll do in college. Still, if you want to go to college, you're stuck with taking one, maybe both, of the tests.

HOW HORRIBLE WILL THE EXPERIENCE BE?

Believe it or not, that's up to you. Some people get woozy just looking at a piece of paper with machine-scorable ovals on it. Even if you're one of those people, being prepared can help to keep your blood pressure in the normal range.

If you can think of these tests as ways to show off how well your mind works, that will help. People who enjoy taking tests tend to do better on them. Of course, telling you to enjoy it is like advising you not to show fear when a snarling dog leaps out at you from an alley. So let's take the snarl out of the experience. The more you know about what you'll be facing and the more prepared you are to face it, the more that snarl will fade.

CAN YOU PREPARE FOR THE SAT I AND THE ACT?

Sure you can. The best way is to spend your academic career studying, doing your homework, and learning what you're supposed to learn. But even if you've done all that, or if it's too late to start doing all that, there are other things you can do. You can spend a lot of money on test preparation courses, though many of them don't help much. You can buy videotapes and computer programs. They may not help much either, but they won't hurt. One of the easiest, most practical, least expensive ways to prepare is to take the tests, over and over again.

The tests are available in libraries and bookstores—old versions that are no longer being administered. Take these tests. They will almost certainly help you. Many experts believe that they will help you more than any computer program, videotape, or "test prep" course in existence.

WHAT'S ON THE TESTS?

What is on the test depends on which one you take. The SAT I contains several sections—three that cover verbal reasoning, three that cover mathematical reasoning, and a seventh section that may cover either. You're not scored on the seventh section, but it may help the test writer develop new tests. (No, they don't pay you for helping them out.) The verbal reasoning part of the SAT I includes analogies, sentence completions, and critical reading. The ACT has four parts—English, mathematics, reading, and science reasoning. The sample passages and questions provided in this material are designed to help you with the reading parts of these tests.

WHAT ARE THE READING TESTS LIKE?

What the SAT I calls "critical reading" and the ACT calls "reading" are very similar. This is the part of each test that presents a reading passage and asks questions about it in order to measure how well you understand what you read. Some of the passages are interesting and well-written. Some are as dry as toast. The trick is to keep reading, no matter what, and have faith in yourself. You don't actually have to understand the passage, you just have to be able to answer the questions asked about it—and that's not as hard as it may seem.

The SAT I and the ACT differ in how many answer choices they provide. (The SAT I has five; the ACT has four.) They differ in what kinds of questions they ask most frequently. (The SAT I tends to emphasize summarizing questions; the ACT tends to emphasize details.) They differ in how they word their questions. But they're really more alike than they are different. Both expect you to be able to understand the meaning of unfamiliar words when the meaning is suggested by the context of the passage. Both expect you to understand what is suggested as well as what is directly stated.

PRACTICE MAKES BETTER

The sample passages and questions in this booklet are designed to provide some practice in dealing with material similar to what you will encounter on the SAT I and ACT reading tests. The sample passages deal with issues relevant to content covered in *World Geography, World History: Patterns of Interaction,* and *The Americans.* This is not what you will find on the SAT I or the ACT. Those tests provide passages from a wide range of sources, both fiction and nonfiction, on a wide variety of subjects, not just history. But these passages are much like the social studies passages you'll find on the real tests.

Because this practice material is modeled on the SAT I and the ACT, it asks similar kinds of questions in similar kinds of ways. However, nobody can write material as much like what you'll find on the real thing as well as the people who write the real thing. So, to repeat a point made earlier, practice as much as you can stand to by taking old tests.

You will notice that some of the passages included here are relatively easy to read and some are relatively difficult. You will find the same thing to be true in the real tests. You will also notice that the questions and their answer choices (particularly the answer choices) are often rather wordy. Both the SAT I and the ACT style their critical reading test material this way. Don't give up; plow through it. Read the question again and again if you need to; eventually it will make sense. Don't let long questions and long answer choices frighten you.

TRICKS OF THE TRADE

People in the testing business call the wrong answers to a test question "distractors." There's a reason for this, and it's one you should know. The wrong answers are written to distract the unknowing test taker. That is, they are deliberately chosen to appeal to people who aren't sure what the correct answer is. In a math test, the wrong answers are often the results of the kinds of math mistakes students most frequently make, so that if you made one of those mistakes, you'll find the answer you came up with among the choices. For a reading test, it's not quite as easy to come up with the distractors, but you can count on this: the test writer tried very hard to make each one look appealing. Don't expect to find many out-and-out ridiculous choices.

Ideally, every time you read a question, you will know immediately what the answer is before you even glance at the answer choices. However, this is the real world, and that won't always happen. Still, the correct answer is there. It's one of the four or five choices that are staring you in the face, and all you have to do is decide which one.

For the critical reading sections in both the SAT I and the ACT, some of the questions are based on material stated in the passage and some require you to "step away" from the passage and make a judgment about it. For the most part, the questions are based on material in the passage; they just might not be based on directly stated information. A surprising number of the questions involve simple restatements of stated material, but even those that go beyond what's stated don't go very far. They simply require you to understand what the passage suggests. If you are asked to infer something, it is because it is implied in the passage. No one can infer something that hasn't been implied, because infer is what a reader or listener does when a writer or speaker implies.

GUESS WHAT!

One of the many nice things about multiple-choice tests is that they give you the right answers. Of course, they hide them in among wrong answers, but it's still better than having to come up with them on your own.

Quick now. What is the capital of Nigeria? Who wrote *The Brothers Karamazov?*

Maybe you're so well-educated that you know the answers to both questions without any assistance. If not, however, here's some help. What is the capital of Nigeria? Is it Berlin, Lagos, Moscow, or Sydney? Who wrote *The Brothers Karamazov?* Feodor Dostoevsky, Mark Twain, Marjorie Kinnan Rawlings, or Pearl Buck?

Why were those questions easier to answer the second time? Because you knew something about every single one of the answer choices. Even if you didn't know the answer for sure before you looked at the answer choices, you probably knew it afterwards. What you knew helped you eliminate the wrong answers and left you with the right ones.

Looking at a group of possible answers to a question makes that question much easier to answer than if you had to pull the answer out of the air. Your only job is to decide which of the answers you're looking at is the right one. That job is even easier when you realize that one way to do it is to decide which of the answers are the wrong ones. That may mean that you're guessing at the correct answer rather than recognizing it, but a correct answer gets the same score whether you knew it for sure or simply guessed it.

The reading sections of the SAT I and ACT do not usually ask simple, factual questions that rely on memory. You will not need to know what general surrendered at Yorktown or who John Foster Dulles was (unless that's what the passage is about). However, the technique of using what you do know to eliminate wrong answer choices will still work.

The ACT has no penalty for guessing. When you don't know the right answer to a question on the ACT, guess!

The SAT I includes a penalty for guessing. If you don't answer a question, you get zero points for that question. If you choose the wrong answer, you get less than zero. A fraction of a point is deducted. This is supposed to keep you from making wild guesses. So, don't make wild guesses. But this doesn't mean you shouldn't guess at all. Don't be scared by that SAT I guessing penalty. Just use your head. If you can eliminate one out of five answer choices (and you usually can), then your chances of choosing the correct answer becomes one out of four. Eliminate another, and your odds improve to one out of three. Look at this mathematically. Guessing can hurt you only if you can't eliminate a single choice and you end up guessing wrong more than 80 percent of the time. The odds are with you.

WHEN THE PASSAGE STUMPS YOU

If you get lost reading the passage, don't give up! As we said before, it may not matter whether you understand the whole thing. All you have to understand are the parts the questions are about, and all you have to understand about them is what correctly answers each question.

Read the passage relatively quickly. Then read each question. A question often points you to a particular paragraph, set of lines, or specific line, and you can read that part of the passage again. If the question asks you to choose the best summary for the third paragraph, concentrate on that paragraph. If the question asks what the word *friable* means in line 47, find it and get a sense of what the passage is talking about there. There may be 19 other hard words in the passage, but so what?

ENOUGH SAID

Try these passages and questions. At the very least, you'll get some additional knowledge about history. At best, you'll get some helpful preparation for the day when you wake up from a good night's sleep, eat a stick-to-your-ribs breakfast, sharpen two No. 2 pencils, and go off to take the real test.

The Spanish, Amerindians, and Smallpox

This passage is from a book that traces the impact of plagues on the history of the world. The passage is followed by questions based on its content. Answer the questions on the basis of what is *stated* or *implied* in the passage.

Wholesale demoralization and simple surrender of will to live certainly played a large part in the destruction of Amerindian communities. Numerous recorded instances of
5 failure to tend newborn babies so that they died unnecessarily, as well as outright suicide, attest to the intensity of Amerindian bewilderment and despair. European military action and harsh treatment of laborers gathered forcibly for some
10 large-scale undertaking also had a role in uprooting and destroying old social structures. But human violence and disregard, however brutal, was not the major factor causing Amerindian populations to melt away as they
15 did. After all, it was not in the interest of the Spaniards and other Europeans to allow potential taxpayers and the Indian work force to diminish. The main destructive role was certainly played by epidemic disease.
20 The first encounter came in 1518 when smallpox reached Hispaniola and attacked the Indian population so virulently that Bartoleme de Las Casas believed only a thousand survived. From Hispaniola, smallpox traveled to Mexico,
25 arriving with the relief expedition that joined [Hernándo] Cortez in 1520. As a result, at the very crisis of the conquest, when Montezuma had been killed and the Aztecs were girding themselves for an attack on the Spaniards, smallpox raged in
30 Tenochtitlán. The leader of the assault, along with innumerable followers, died within hours of compelling the Spaniards to retreat from their city. Instead of following up on the initial success and harrying the tiny band of Spaniards from the
35 land, therefore, as might have been expected had the smallpox not paralyzed effective action, the Aztecs lapsed into a stunned inactivity. Cortez thus was able to rally his forces, gather allies from among the Aztecs' subject peoples, and return for
40 the final siege and destruction of the capital.
Clearly, if smallpox had not come when it did, the Spanish victory could not have been achieved in Mexico. The same was true of [Francisco] Pizarro's filibuster into Peru. For the smallpox
45 epidemic in Mexico did not confine its ravages to

Aztec territory. Instead, it spread to Guatemala, where it appeared in 1520, and continued southward, penetrating the Inca domain in 1525 or 1526. Consequences there were just as drastic
50 as among the Aztecs. The reigning Inca died of the disease while away from his capital on campaign in the North. His designated heir also died, leaving no legitimate successor. Civil war ensued, and it was amid this wreckage of the Inca
55 political structure that Pizarro and his crew of roughnecks made their way to Cuzco and plundered its treasures. He met no serious military resistance at all.
Two points seem particularly worth
60 emphasizing here. First, Spaniards and Indians readily agreed that epidemic disease was a particularly dreadful and unambiguous form of divine punishment. Interpretation of pestilence as a sign of God's displeasure was a part of the
65 Spanish inheritance, enshrined in the Old Testament and in the whole Christian tradition. The Amerindians, lacking all experience of anything remotely like the initial series of lethal epidemics, concurred. Their religious doctrines
70 recognized that superhuman power lodged in deities whose behavior toward men was often angry. It was natural, therefore, for them to assign an unexampled effect to a supernatural cause, quite apart from the Spanish missionary efforts
75 that urged the same interpretation of the catastrophe upon dazed and demoralized converts.
Secondly, the Spaniards were nearly immune from the terrible disease that raged so mercilessly
80 among the Indians. They had almost always been exposed in childhood and so developed effective immunity. Given the interpretation of the cause of pestilence accepted by both parties, such a manifestation of divine partiality for the invaders
85 was conclusive. The gods of Aztecs as much as the

GO ON TO THE NEXT PAGE

God of the Christians seemed to agree that the white newcomers had divine approval for all they did. And while God thus seemed to favor the whites, regardless of their morality and piety or
90 lack thereof, his wrath was visited upon the Indians with an unrelenting harshness that often puzzled and distressed the Christian missionaries who soon took charge of the moral and religious life of their converts along the frontiers of Spain's
95 American dominions.

1. According to the author, newborn Amerindian babies often died as a result of

   (A) their parents' surrender to despair
   (B) exposure to European diseases
   (C) attempts to appease the deities
   (D) the suicides of traditional caregivers
   (E) European military action

2. The passage suggests that Pizarro was able to easily conquer the Inca because

   (A) most Inca forces were wiped out by disease
   (B) disease left the Inca without strong leadership
   (C) civil war destroyed much of the Inca population
   (D) the Inca leader was absent on another campaign
   (E) the Inca had lost the will to live

3. Just before an outbreak of smallpox among the Aztec, they had

   (A) laid siege to Tenochtitlán
   (B) moved south into Guatemala
   (C) attempted to invade Hispaniola
   (D) retreated from Tenochtitlán
   (E) driven the Spanish from Tenochtitlán

4. In line 44, "filibuster" most nearly means

   (A) a hostile expedition
   (B) a delaying tactic
   (C) a revolutionary effort
   (D) a courageous advance
   (E) an attempt to spread infection

5. The passage suggests that Spanish brutality was limited by

   (A) Christian religious beliefs
   (B) an outbreak of infectious diseases
   (C) a desire to have a productive work force
   (D) a lack of large-scale weapons of destruction
   (E) weakness in their own forces caused by disease

6. The Spaniards' immunity to smallpox was seen at the time as evidence

   (A) that they were deities
   (B) that God favored them
   (C) of their superior morality
   (D) of the benefits of early exposure
   (E) of superior physical fitness

7. The passage suggests that Spanish missionaries were confused by what they viewed as

   (A) God's anger at Amerindian groups
   (B) Amerindian reluctance to be converted
   (C) immorality and lack of piety among the Spanish
   (D) God's preference for Christians over other groups
   (E) their inability to control the religious lives of their converts

8. In line 62, the author uses the word "unambiguous" to note that divine punishment was seen as

   (A) devastating
   (B) unmistakable
   (C) undeserved
   (D) effective
   (E) just

9. According to the author, which of the following did the Amerindians and the Spanish agree about?

   I. Disease was a type of divine punishment.
   II. The actions of the Spanish met with divine approval.
   III. The Christian God was more powerful than the gods of the Aztecs.

   (A) I only
   (B) II only
   (C) III only
   (D) I and II only
   (E) I, II, and III

READING TEST

Creating a Nation

15 Minutes

DIRECTIONS: After reading the following passage, choose the best
answer to each question and circle the letter of that answer.

SOCIAL STUDIES: This passage is adapted from
*Witnesses at the Creation: Hamilton, Madison,
Jay, and the Constitution* (©1985 by Richard B.
Morris).

Looking back on the years between
the Revolution and the convening of the
Constitutional Convention, Dr. Benjamin Rush,
physician, philosopher, and a signer of the
5 Declaration of Independence, observed that "there
is nothing more common than to confound the
term American Revolution with that of the late
American War. The American War is over, but
this is far from being the case with the American
10 Revolution. On the contrary, but the first act of
the great drama is closed."

Having played conspicuous roles in the first
act of that three-act drama, covering the years
from 1776–1789, Hamilton, Jay, and Madison,
15 joined forces with other like-minded nationalist
leaders in wrestling with the issues and conflicts
played out in the second act. These included
constitutional change, legal and social reform, and
economic recovery to bring to maturity the
20 splendid fruits of peace.

The thirteen states seemed to these leaders to
be a nation of paradox. America's territory had
been more than doubled by the peace, making it
the largest republic in world history, one that did
25 not, like Rome, turn into an empire. Its population
had grown at a faster rate than ever before, or
even thereafter. From less than two and a half
million people at the end of the war, a wave of
European immigration and a postwar population
30 explosion combined to give the new country close
to four million inhabitants by 1790. Included in
this figure were seven hundred thousand black
slaves and an additional sixty thousand free
blacks. The North was initiating notable steps
35 toward bringing about black emancipation, but
in the South, save for individual cases of
manumission, slavery remained untouchable.

Equality, so eloquently proclaimed in the Great
40 Declaration, proved a most elusive goal in a society
resting upon slavery and indentured servitude and
among a people for whom farming was the chief
occupation. Agriculture claimed the attention of
great estate holders, of small freeholders, of
45 subsistence farmers, and of a rising tenancy. Free
white labor competed in many areas with slavery,
that "dark gloominess hanging over the land," as
the Quaker leader and antislavery advocate John
Woolman described it, while women enjoyed no
50 political rights and suffered an inferior position at
law, and Indians were considered a breed apart. A
minority formed an affluent society, including the
nouveaux riches who had exploited the late war's
opportunities to their own profit. Another
55 minority was mired in poverty. Between was a
large middling group, by no means untouched by
the postwar business depression, but comfortably
optimistic in a society that was evidencing more
upward mobility and less stratification than any
60 nation of the Old World.

If social, cultural, regional, sectional, and racial
divisions kept the American people from
effectively uniting, difficulties in communication
conspired to discourage close physical contact
65 among people in isolated areas. It took six days for
a stagecoach to make the journey between New
York and Boston, and more than three between
Philadelphia and New York, a mere ninety miles.
Innumerable rivers had to be forded by ferries.
70 Save for the span across the Charles River, no
significant river had been bridged prior to the
convening of the delegates to the Constitutional
Convention in Philadelphia in 1787. Hence,
engineers and businessmen joined forces in plans
75 for improving inland navigation through the
construction of locks, canals, and bridges, and
inventors put steam engines in small craft in
efforts to sail upriver.

As Hamilton, Jay, and Madison saw it, the
80 disunity of the country could be put down

primarily to the weak constitutional structure. The Articles of Confederation were finally ratified in 1781 by the holdout state of Maryland after Virginia, along with other states, had ceded her
90 western land claims to Congress. The prestige of that body had fallen so low that some states no longer bothered to send delegates. Its presidency was taken so lightly that John Hancock, elected to that position in 1785 (he had, of course, served in
95 that capacity years earlier and signed his name in bold letters to the Declaration), never bothered to come to New York for its sessions. The men who later sat in Congress were, with few exceptions, hardly noteworthy.

1. The quotation from Benjamin Rush (lines 5–11) maintains that the American War differs from the American Revolution in that the revolution:

  A. had begun long before the war.
  B. continued long after the war.
  C. was, in reality, more dramatic than the war.
  D. suffered from disunity, while the war was a unified struggle.

2. According to the author, the American way of life in the late 1700s made it difficult to:

  F. remain optimistic.
  G. accept and embrace immigrants.
  H. make equality a reality.
  J. separate people into social classes.

3. Most advances in transportation in the late 1700s involved travel by:

  A. boat.   **C.** railroad.
  B. stagecoach.   **D.** horseback.

4. According to the fifth paragraph, communication was hindered by:

  F. political conspiracies.
  G. the enormous size of the new nation.
  H. difficulties involved in transportation.
  J. divisions among the American people.

5. As it is used in line 37, the word *manumission* means:

  A. an inspiring example.   **C.** hard labor.
  B. a serious debate.   **D.** a freeing from slavery.

6. The passage suggests that John Hancock failed to attend sessions of Congress because:

  F. it was so difficult to get to them.
  G. he viewed his position as unimportant.
  H. he disagreed with the men who held office.
  J. his state did not bother to send delegates.

7. According to this passage, the group that viewed its situation in life as likely to change for the better was:

  A. the lower class.   **C.** the *nouveau riches.*
  B. the middle class.   **D.** the established upper class.

8. Based on information in this passage, it is most likely that the phrase *the second act* in line 17 refers to:

  F. the Revolutionary War period.
  G. the Constitutional Convention.
  H. the time between the Declaration of Independence and 1789.
  J. the time between the war and the Constitutional Convention.

9. The phrase *enjoyed no political rights* (lines 49–50) means that women:

  A. did not have the benefit of any political rights.
  B. did not, at that time, wish to change their political situation.
  C. had only those political rights that they did not want.
  D. had few political rights, which they did not exercise.

10. This passage uses the word *Congress* to refer to:

  F. the legislative bodies of the thirteen states as a group.
  G. the legislative body formed by the U.S. Constitution.
  H. the men who signed the Declaration of Independence.
  J. the national government under the Articles of Confederation.

11. This passage focuses primarily on which of the following?

  A. Physical barriers to effective communication
  B. Obstacles to achieving unity in the new nation
  C. Weaknesses caused by a lack of effective leadership
  D. The new nation's lofty goals

12. Is the following sentence (lines 70–73) treated in the passage as an established fact?

  Save for the span across the Charles River, no significant river had been bridged prior to the convening of the delegates to the Constitutional Convention in Philadelphia in 1787.

  F. No, because the word *significant* suggests a personal judgment.
  G. No, because it is the author's inference from the attendance records of other meetings.
  H. Yes, because whether or not bridges existed is verifiable.
  J. Yes, because the date of the Constitutional Convention is a matter of record.

Plantation Slavery

This passage is from a book by two noted historians about African Americans up until the abolition of slavery. The passage is followed by questions based on its content. Answer the questions on the basis of what is *stated* or *implied* in the passage.

Plantation slavery, as it developed in the cotton kingdom, was something of an anomaly on the American frontier. Although slavery was almost as old as the permanent settlements in
5 America, not until the nineteenth century did it occupy so much of the attention and energy of the settlers as to threaten other forms of labor. The frontier had been a place where one could make or lose a fortune largely by one's own
10 labors. The emergence of the great cotton plantation introduced a kind of exploitation of human and natural resources and fostered a type of discipline in rural areas that created what could at best be called a peculiar situation. Indeed, every
15 aspect of agricultural life in the Southern United States underwent a complete transformation as a result of the new economic and social forces let loose by the Industrial Revolution. And what the Industrial Revolution did to the capitalistic
20 system, new lands and the prospect of wealth from cotton culture did to the system of slavery. Large-scale operations were the order of the day. The farm became a plantation, which in turn became a rural factory with the impersonality of a
25 large-scale economic organization. The face of the Southern frontier had been changed. Cotton and slavery were the great transforming forces. . . .

The impression should not be conveyed that the whites of the South, numbering about 8
30 million in 1860, generally enjoyed the fruits of slave labor. There was a remarkable concentration of the slave population in the hands of a relative few. In 1860 there were only 384,884 slave owners. Thus, fully three-fourths of the white
35 people of the South had neither slaves nor an immediate economic interest in the maintenance of slavery or the plantation system. And yet, the institution came to dominate the political and economic thinking of the entire South and to
40 shape its social pattern for two principal reasons. The great majority of the staple crops were produced on plantations employing slave labor, thus giving the owners an influence out of proportion to their number. Then, there was the
45 hope on the part of most nonslaveholders that they would some day become owners of slaves.

Consequently, they took on the habits and patterns of thought of slaveholders before they actually joined that select class.
50 While slaves were concentrated in areas where the staple crops were produced on a large scale, the bulk of the slave owners were small farmers. . . . More than 200,000 owners in 1860 had five slaves or less. Fully 338,000 owners, or 88
55 percent of all the owners of slaves in 1860, held less than twenty slaves. (One must not be misled by these figures, however, for over one-half of the slaves were employed as field workers on plantations with holdings of more than twenty
60 slaves, and at least 25 percent of the slave community lived on plantations where the number of slaves was in excess of fifty.) It is fairly generally conceded that from thirty to sixty slaves constituted the most profitable agricultural unit.
65 If that is true, there were fewer plantations in the South that had what might be considered a satisfactory working force than has been generally believed. The concentration of 88 percent of all slaveholders in the small slave-owning group is
70 significant for several important reasons. In the first place, it emphasizes the fact that the influence of large owners must have been enormous, since they have been successful in impressing posterity with the erroneous
75 conception that plantations on which there were large numbers of slaves were typical. In the second place, it brings out the fact that the majority of slaveholding was carried on by yeomen rather than gentry. Finally, in a study of
80 the institution of slavery, there is a rather strong indication that some distinction should be made between the possession of one or two slaves and the possession of, say, fifty or more.

GO ON TO THE NEXT PAGE ⟩

1. The statement in lines 25–26 that "The face of the Southern frontier had been changed" refers to a switch from

   (A) small farms to large plantations
   (B) antislavery to proslavery views
   (C) self-reliance to interdependence
   (D) agriculture to manufacturing
   (E) a loose social structure to a rigid one

2. Which generalization about the South before the Civil War do the authors claim is inaccurate?

   (A) Most Southerners supported slavery.
   (B) Most cotton was raised on large plantations.
   (C) Plantations with many slaves were typical.
   (D) The production of cotton dominated the South economically.
   (E) Slaveholders controlled Southern politics.

3. What does the passage give as the major reason for why nonslaveholding Southerners supported slavery?

   (A) They resented interference from Northerners.
   (B) They wanted to protect the economic interests of the region.
   (C) They hoped to become slaveholders themselves.
   (D) The existence of slavery kept them from occupying the lowest social class.
   (E) Slavery had allowed the settlement of the Southern frontier.

4. In line 79, the word "yeomen" is used to mean

   (A) servants
   (B) slaveholders
   (C) landowners
   (D) members of the highest social class
   (E) people of moderate social standing

5. According to this passage, the main reason that some white Southerners did not own slaves was that they

   (A) did not grow cotton
   (B) respected self-reliance
   (C) had a moral objection to slavery
   (D) couldn't afford to own slaves
   (E) lived on the Southern frontier

6. It can be determined from this passage that the states that produced the most cotton also had the most

   (A) slaves
   (B) slaveholders
   (C) slaveholders with fewer than five slaves
   (D) slaveholders with more than twenty slaves
   (E) slaveholders with more than fifty slaves

7. By the beginning of the Civil War, approximately what percent of all slaveholders owned more than twenty slaves?

   (A) 12 percent
   (B) 25 percent
   (C) 50 percent
   (D) 75 percent
   (E) 88 percent

READING TEST

Differences Between American and European Farmers

15 Minutes

DIRECTIONS: After reading the following passage, choose the best
answer to each question and circle the letter of that answer.

SOCIAL SCIENCE: This passage is adapted from Richard Hofstadter's work *The Age of Reform* (©1955 by Richard Hofstadter). The passage discusses some differences between the lifestyles and practices of American and European farmers.

The penchant for speculation and the lure of new and different lands bred in the American farmer a tremendous passion for moving—and not merely, as one common view would have it,
5 on the part of those who had failed, but also on the part of those who had succeeded. For farmers who had made out badly, the fresh lands may have served on occasion as a safety valve, but for others who had made out well enough on a
10 speculative basis, or who were beginning a farming "career," it was equally a risk valve—an opportunity to exploit the full possibilities of the great American land bubble. Mobility among farmers had serious effects upon an agricultural
15 tradition never noted for careful cultivation: in a nation whose soil is notoriously heterogeneous, farmers too often had little chance to get to know the quality of their land; they failed to plan and manure and replenish; they neglected
20 diversification for the one-crop system and ready cash. There was among them little attachment to land or locality; instead there developed the false euphoria of local "boosting," encouraged by the railroads, land companies, and farmers
25 themselves; in place of village contacts and communal spirit based upon ancestral attachments, there was professional optimism based upon hopes for a quick rise in values.

In a very real and profound sense, then, the
30 United States failed to develop (except in some localities, chiefly in the East) a distinctly *rural* culture. If a rural culture means an emotional and craftsmanlike dedication to the soil, a traditional and pre-capitalistic outlook, a tradition-directed
35 rather than a career-directed type of character, and a village community devoted to ancestral ways and habitually given to communal action, then the prairies and plains never had one. . . .

Immigrant farmers, who really were yeomen
40 with a background of genuine agrarian values, were frequently bewildered at the ethos of American agriculture. Marcus Hansen points out: "The ambition of the German-American father, for instance, was to see his sons on reaching
45 manhood established with their families on farms clustered about his own. To take complete possession of a township with sons, sons-in-law and nephews was not an unrealizable ideal. To this end the would-be patriarch dedicated all his
50 plodding industry. One by one, he bought adjacent farms, the erstwhile owners joining the current to the farther West. Heavily timbered acres and swamp lands which had been lying unused were prepared for cultivation by patient
55 and unceasing toil. . . . But the American father made no such efforts on behalf of his offspring. To be a self-made man was his ideal. He had come in as a 'first settler' and had created a farm with his ax; let the boys do the same. One of them
60 perhaps was kept at home as a helper to his aging parents; the rest set out to achieve beyond the mountains or beyond the river what the father had accomplished in the West of his day. Thus mobility was fostered by family policy." The
70 continuing influx of immigrants, ready to settle on cleared and slightly improved land, greatly facilitated the Yankee race across the continent.

American agriculture was also distinguishable from European agriculture in the kind of rural life
75 . . . it sustained. . . . In Europe land was limited and dear, while labor was abundant and relatively cheap; in America this ration between land and labor was inverted. In Europe small farmers lived in villages, where generations of the same family
80 were reared upon the same soil, and where careful cultivation and the minute elimination of waste were necessary to support a growing population on a limited amount of land. Endless and patient labor, including the labor of peasant women and
85 children exploited to a degree to which the Yankee would not go except under the stress of pioneering conditions, was available to conserve and tailor the

land and keep it fertile. On limited plots cultivated
by an ample labor force, the need for machinery
90 was not urgent, and hence the demand for liquid
capital in large amounts was rare. Diversification,
self-sufficiency, and the acceptance of a low
standard of living also contributed to hold down
this demand. Much managerial skill was required
95 for such an agricultural regime, but it was the skill
of the craftsman and the traditional tiller of the
soil. Village life provided a community and a
cooperative milieu, a pooling of knowledge and
lore, a basis of common action to minimize risks.

100   In America the greater availability of land and
the scarcity of labor made for extensive agriculture,
which was wasteful of the soil, and placed a pre-
mium on machines to bring large tracts under cultivation. His demand for expensive machinery, his
105 expectation of higher standards of living, and his
tendency to go into debt to acquire extensive
acreage created an urgent need for cash and
tempted the farmer into capitalizing more and
more on his greatest single asset: the unearned
110 appreciation in the value of his land. The managerial skill required for success under these conditions was as much businesslike as craftsmanlike.
The predominance in American agriculture of the
isolated farmstead standing in the midst of great
115 acreage, the frequent movements, the absence of
village life, deprived the farmer and his family of
the advantages of community, lowered the chances
of association and co-operation, and encouraged
that rampant, suspicious, and almost suicidal indi-
120 vidualism for which the American farmer was long
noted and which organizations like the Grange
tried to combat. The characteristic product of
American rural society was not a yeoman or a village, but a harassed little country businessman who
125 worked very hard, moved all too often, gambled
with his land, and made his way alone.

1. In line 16, the author describes American soil as
"notoriously heterogeneous" to convey the idea that
the quality of American soil:

A. was unusually high.
B. was unusually poor.
C. deteriorated rapidly under abuse.
D. varied widely from region to region.

2. According to the passage, which of the following is
necessary for the development of a "distinctly *rural
culture*" (lines 31–32)?

I. A communal spirit
II. Respect for tradition
III. Fresh lands to serve as a risk valve

F. I only
G. I and II only
H. II and III only
J. I, II, and III

3. The passage suggests that when German-American
farmers bought neighboring farms in America, their
chief motivation was:

A. to increase the value of their land holdings.
B. to protect the investment they had originally
made.
C. to allow for the creation of a family-based
community.
D. to provide the opportunity for greater crop
diversification.

4. The passage suggests that a sense of community
can develop in rural places only if there is:

F. little cultural diversity.
G. great cultural diversity.
H. a high demand for labor.
J. a sense of stability and constancy.

5. According to the passage, all of the following
conditions contributed to the careful cultivation of
European farmlands EXCEPT:

A. the practice of buying adjacent farmlands.
B. the managerial skill of farmers.
C. the abundance of cheap labor.
D. the scarcity of land.

6. According to the passage, the most important factor
in determining an American farmer's mobility was
which of the following?

F. The farmer's age
G. The farmer's experience
H. The farmer's traditional values
J. The farmer's degree of success

7. In this passage, the author views the independent
streak of native-born farmers as a:

A. complete mystery.
B. trait common to all Americans.
C. logical result of their mode of life.
D. trait deeply rooted in European agricultural
practices.

8. According to the passage, the abundance of land
and the scarcity of agricultural labor on the frontier
led to which of the following?

I. A need for machinery
II. A need for liquid capital
III. Cultivation of extensive tracts of land
IV. A habitual reliance on communal action

F. I and III only   H. I, II, and III only
G. II and III only   J. I, II, III, and IV

Wilson, Neutrality, and Intervention

The passage below is followed by questions based on its content. Answer the questions on the basis of what is *stated* or *implied* in the passage and in any introductory material that may be provided.

When World War I began in Europe, President Woodrow Wilson, who had been elected on the strength of his Progressive principles, pledged to keep the United States neutral. The reversal of his position had serious consequences for the nation as well as for the Progressive movement.

In the course of the long struggle over neutrality Wilson is the key figure, not merely because of the central power of leadership he exercised but because he was, on this issue, a
5   representative American and a good Progressive citizen who expressed in every inconsistency, every vacillation, every reluctance, the predominant feelings of the country. He embodied, too, the triumph of the Progressive need to phrase the
10   problems of national policy in moral terms. At first, while sharing the common reluctance to become involved in the struggle, he eschewed the "realistic" formula that the whole struggle was none of America's business and that the essence of the
15   American problem was to stay out at all costs. Even his plea for neutrality was pitched in high moral terms: the nation must stay out in order to be of service, to provide a center of sanity uncorrupted by the strains and hatreds of belligerence. . . .
20   Then, as the country drew closer to involvement under the pressure of events, Wilson again chose the language of idealism to formulate the American problem—the problem not only whether the United States should intervene, but
25   what might be the valid reasons for intervening. One view . . . rested chiefly upon the national interest and cool calculations of the future advantage of the United States. According to this view, a victory for imperial Germany would
30   represent a threat to the long-term interests of the United States in some sense that a victory for the Allies would not. It was expected that a victorious Germany would be more aggressive, more formidable, more anti-American, and that after the
35   defeat of the Allies and the surrender of the British fleet it would either turn upon the United States at some future time or at least present so forceful and continuous a threat as to compel this country to remain a perpetual armed camp in order to protect its security. Therefore, it was argued, it was the
40   business of the United States, as a matter of self-interest to see to it that the Allies were not defeated—acting if possible as a nonbelligerent, but if necessary as a belligerent. Another view was
45   that intervention in the war could not properly be expressed in such calculating and self-regarding terms, but must rest upon moral and ideological considerations—the defense of international law and freedom of the seas, the rights of small
50   nations, the fight against autocracy and militarism, the struggle to make the world safe for democracy. To be sure, the argument from self-preservation and national interest and the argument from morals and ideals were not mutually contradictory,
55   and both tended to have a place in the course of public discussion. But Wilson's course, the characteristically Progressive course, was to minimize and subordinate the self-regarding considerations, and to place American intervention
60   upon the loftiest possible plane. He committed himself to this line of action quite early in the game when he rested so much of his diplomacy on the issue of the conduct of German submarine warfare and the freedom of the seas. This
65   was quixotically formulated because it linked the problem of American intervention or non-intervention to an issue of international law—though one entirely congenial to the Progressive concern over lawlessness. To Wilson's critics it
70   seemed hypocritical because in purely formal terms British violations of maritime law were about as serious as German violations. American concern over them could never be pressed so vigorously because such a course of action would
75   trip over the more urgent desire to do nothing to impair the chances of Allied victory. . . .
Not long after they began to pay the price of war, the [American] people began to feel that they had been gulled by its promoters both among
80   the Allies and in the United States. . . . The war purged the pent-up guilts, shattered the ethos of

GO ON TO THE NEXT PAGE

responsibility that had permeated the rhetoric of more than a decade. It convinced the people that they had paid the price for such comforts of modern life as they could claim, that they had

85 finally answered to the full the Progressive demand for sacrifice and self-control and altruism. In repudiating Wilson, the treaty, the League [of Nations], and the war itself, they repudiated the Progressive rhetoric and the Progressive mood—

90 for it was Wilson himself and his propagandists who had done so much to tie all these together. . . . The reaction went farther than this: it destroyed the popular impulse that had sustained Progressive politics for well over a decade before 1914. The

95 pressure for civic participation was followed by widespread apathy, the sense of responsibility by neglect, the call for sacrifice by hedonism.

1. The author feels that Wilson's struggle with neutrality was mainly a struggle with his

   (A) ego or pride
   (B) past experiences
   (C) political opponents
   (D) sense of patriotic duty
   (E) intellect and conscience

2. The "realistic" (line 13) point of view held that America should stay out of the war because

   (A) the war was evil
   (B) the war was a European matter
   (C) public opinion was strongly antiwar
   (D) both sides had violated maritime laws
   (E) America wasn't prepared to fight a war

3. In this passage, the author chiefly characterizes the Progressives during the years before the war as being

   (A) rigid
   (B) logical
   (C) idealistic
   (D) insincere
   (E) compassionate

4. In line 12, "eschewed" most nearly means

   (A) avoided
   (B) stressed
   (C) faced up to
   (D) understood
   (E) contradicted

5. The author suggests that using an issue of international law to justify American intervention in the war was Wilson's way of

   (A) inspiring the American people to support the war effort
   (B) attempting to limit the scope of American involvement in the war
   (C) answering critics who accused him of showing a lack of concern over lawlessness
   (D) making American involvement seem consistent with idealism rather than self-interest
   (E) convincing the American people of the threat they faced from a potential German victory

6. In the last paragraph, the author argues that Progressivism was ultimately undone by its

   (A) early support of neutrality
   (B) association with an unpopular war
   (C) excessive demands for self-sacrifice
   (D) rejection of the realities of modern life
   (E) inability to wholeheartedly support the war

7. In the last sentence, the author uses a series of contrasts to show

   (A) what should have been versus what was
   (B) how Americans became divided by the war
   (C) how American attitudes and behavior changed
   (D) the conflict between morality and practicality
   (E) the realities that lay behind Progressive propaganda

READING TEST

Causes and Effects of the Great Depression

15 Minutes

DIRECTIONS: After reading the following passage, choose the best
answer to each question and circle the letter of that answer.

SOCIAL SCIENCE: This passage is adapted from
The Perils of Prosperity, 1914–32 by William E.
Leuchtenburg (©1958 by The University of
Chicago). The passage discusses some of the
causes and effects of the Great Depression.

The prosperity of the 1920s had been founded
on construction and the automobile industry.
Residential construction, which had stood at five
billion dollars in 1925, was down to three billion
5 by 1929. The automobile industry continued to
grow, but after 1925, it grew at a much slower
rate, cutting back purchases of steel and other
material; the cycle of events, whereby an increase
in car production produces rapid increases in
10 steel, rubber, glass, and other industries, now
operated in a reverse manner to speed the
country toward a major depression. By 1929 the
automobile industry—and satellites like the
rubber-tire business—were badly overbuilt. Since
15 there was no new industry to take the place of
automobiles and no policy of federal spending to
provide new investment . . . , it was inevitable
that as investment fell off and the rate of
production slackened in the key industries, a
20 serious recession would result.

There was no single cause of the [1929 stock
market] crash and the ensuing depression, but
much of the responsibility for both falls on the
foolhardy assumption that the special interests of
25 business and the national interest were identical.
Management had siphoned off gains in
productivity in high profits, while the farmer got
less, and the worker, though better off, received
wage increases disproportionately small when
30 compared to profits. As a result the purchasing
power of workers and farmers was not great
enough to sustain prosperity. For a time this
was partly obscured by the fact that consumers
bought goods on installment at a rate faster than
35 their income was expanding, but it was inevitable
that a time would come when they would have to
reduce purchases, and the cutback in buying
would sap the whole economy.

With no counteraction from labor unions,
40 which were weak, or from government, which had
no independent policy, business increased profits
at twice the rate of the growth in productivity. So
great were profits that many corporations no
longer needed to borrow, and as a result Federal
45 Reserve banks had only minimal control over
speculation. With no other outlet, profits were
plunged into the stock market, producing
runaway speculation.

The policies of the federal government in the
50 1920s were disastrous. Its tax policies made the
maldistribution of income and oversaving by the
rich still more serious. . . . Its monetary policies
were irresponsible; at critical junctures, the fiscal
policy of the Coolidge administration moved in
55 precisely the wrong direction. The administration
took the narrow interests of business groups
to be the national interest, and the result was
catastrophic.

The market crash played a major role in
60 precipitating the Great Depression. It shattered
business confidence, ruined many investors, and
wiped out holding company and investment trust
structures. It destroyed an important source of
long-term capital and sharply cut back consumer
65 demand. Yet business would have been able to
weather even the shock of the crash, if business
had been fundamentally sound. The crash
exposed the weaknesses that underlay the
prosperous economy of the twenties—the over-
70 expansion of major industries, the maldistribution
of income, the weak banking structure, and the
overdependence of the economy on consumer
durable goods.

During the 1920s almost seven thousand
75 banks failed; no industrial nation in the world
had as unstable and as irresponsible a banking
system as the United States. "The banks," noted
one writer, "provided everything for their
customers but a roulette wheel." In the 1920s
80 wrote Professor Schumpeter, "a new type of bank

executive emerged who had little of the banker and looked much like a bond salesman"; the new type of banker-promoter financed speculation and loaded the banks with dubious assets. Nothing did
85 more to turn the stock market crash of 1929 into a prolonged depression than the destruction of business and public morale by the failure of the banks.

A year after the crash, six million men walked
90 the streets looking for work. By 1932, there were 660,000 jobless in Chicago, a million in New York City. In heavily industrialized cities the toll of the depression read, as one observer noted, like British casualty lists at the Somme—so awesome as to
95 become in the end meaningless, for the sheer statistics numbed the mind. . . . In the three years after the crash, 100,000 workers were fired on the average every week.

By 1932, the physical output of manufacturing
100 had fallen to 54 per cent of what it had been in 1929; it was a shade less than production in 1913. All the gains of the golden twenties were wiped out in a few months. By the last year of the Hoover administration, the automobile industry was
105 operating at only one-fifth of its 1929 capacity. As the great auto plants in Detroit lay idle, fires were banked in the steel furnaces on the Allegheny and the Mahoning. By the summer of 1932, steel plants operated at 12 per cent of capacity . . .

110 The farmer, who had seen little of the prosperity of the 1920s, was devastated by the depression. The crash—and the ensuing financial debacle—destroyed much of what remained of his foreign markets. American foreign trade declined
115 from $10 billion in 1929 to $3 billion in 1932. . . . As foreign nations erected new barriers to American products and unemployment cut heavily into the domestic market, crop prices skidded to new lows. . . . The result was catastrophic. Gross
120 farm income fell from nearly $12 billion to the pitiful sum of $5 billion.

1. The quotation in lines 77–79 is used by the author to illustrate the point that:

  A. banks weren't taking customer service seriously.
  B. banks were desperate to attract new customers.
  C. banks were encouraging consumers to gamble with their money.
  D. consumers were being offered more banking choices than ever before.

2. It can reasonably be inferred from the passage that, in the 1920s, government worked primarily for the benefit of:

  F. farmers.   **H.** unionized workers.
  G. business   **J.** non-unionized workers.

3. According to the passage, the average worker in the mid-1920s was:

  A. earning less than ever before.
  B. saving more than he or she was spending.
  C. spending more than he or she was making.
  D. investing too heavily in the stock market.

4. According to the passage, part of the problem with business profits in the 1920s was that they:

  F. made labor unions weak.
  G. failed to keep up with wages.
  H. encouraged stock market speculation.
  J. encouraged consumers to buy on installment.

5. According to the author, the stock market crash:

  A. had no effect on the Great Depression.
  B. was the only cause of the Great Depression.
  C. was the main cause of the Great Depression.
  D. was one of the causes of the Great Depression.

6. According to the passage, the economy of the 1920s would have been more stable if:

  I. wages had been distributed more evenly.
  II. the wealthy had put more income into savings.
  III. business productivity had matched business profits.

  F. I and II only   **H.** II and III only
  G. I and III only   **J.** I, II, and III

7. The author believes that the economic situation of the 1920s would have been improved if:

  A. major industries had expanded.
  B. wages had increased less rapidly.
  C. more people had invested in stocks.
  D. income had been distributed more equally.

8. According to the passage, the Great Depression caused:

  I. high rates of inflation.
  II. high rates of unemployment.
  III. a decrease in world trade.
  IV. runaway speculation in the stock market.

  F. I and II only   **H.** III and IV only
  G. II and III only   **J.** I, II, III, and IV

9. In the first paragraph, the author suggests that "a serious recession would result" from decreases in all of the following EXCEPT:

  A. retail prices of new automobiles.
  B. consumer demand for automobiles.
  C. the number of automobiles being produced.
  D. residential construction.

The Atomic Bomb

The passage below is followed by questions based on its content. Answer the questions on the basis of what is *stated* or *implied* in the passage and in any introductory material that may be provided.

On August 6, 1945, the United States dropped, on the Japanese city of Hiroshima, the first atomic bomb used in warfare. Three days later, a second bomb was dropped on Nagasaki. This passage conveys the thoughts of Winston Churchill, the prime minister of Great Britain, upon learning of the first successful test explosion of the atomic bomb on July 17, 1945.

On July 17 world-shaking news arrived. In the afternoon Stimson called at my abode and laid before me a sheet of paper on which was written, "Babies satisfactorily born." By his manner I saw

5 something extraordinary had happened. "It means," he said, "that the experiment in the Mexican desert has come off. The atomic bomb is a reality." Although we had followed this dire quest with every scrap of information imparted to

10 us, we had not been told beforehand, or at any rate I did not know, the date of the decisive trial. No responsible scientist would predict what would happen when the first full-scale atomic explosion was tried. Were these bombs useless or

15 were they annihilating? Now we knew. The "babies" had been "satisfactorily born." No one could yet measure the immediate military consequences of the discovery . . .

Next morning a plane arrived with a full

20 description of this tremendous event in the human story. Stimson brought me the report. I tell the tale as I recall it. The bomb, or its equivalent, had been detonated at the top of a pylon one hundred feet high. Everyone had been

25 cleared away for ten miles round, and the scientists and their staffs crouched behind massive concrete shields and shelters at about that distance. The blast had been terrific. An enormous column of flame and smoke shot up to

30 the fringe of the atmosphere of our poor earth. Devastation inside a one-mile circle was absolute. Here then was a speedy end to the Second World War, and perhaps to much else besides.

[President Truman] invited me to confer with

35 him forthwith. . . . Up to this moment we had shaped our ideas towards an assault upon the homeland of Japan by terrific air bombing and by the invasion of very large armies. We had contemplated the desperate resistance of the

40 Japanese fighting to the death with Samurai devotion, not only in pitched battles, but in every cave and dugout. I had in my mind the spectacle of Okinawa island, where many thousands of Japanese, rather than surrender, had drawn up in

45 line and destroyed themselves by hand-grenades after their leaders had solemnly performed the rite of hara-kiri. To quell the Japanese resistance man by man and conquer the country yard by yard might well require the loss of a million American

50 lives and half that number of British—or more if we could get them there: for we were resolved to share the agony. Now all this nightmare picture had vanished. In its place was the vision—fair and bright indeed it seemed—of the end of the whole

55 war in one or two violent shocks. I thought immediately myself of how the Japanese people, whose courage I had always admired, might find in the apparition of this almost supernatural weapon an excuse which would save their honour

60 and release them from their obligation of being killed to the last fighting man.

Moreover, we should not need the Russians. The end of the Japanese war no longer depended upon the pouring in of their armies for the final

65 and perhaps protracted slaughter. We had no need to ask favours of them. The array of European problems could therefore be faced on their merits and according to the broad principles of the United Nations. We seemed suddenly to have become

70 possessed of a merciful abridgment of the slaughter in the East and of a far happier prospect in Europe. I have no doubt that these thoughts were present in the minds of my American friends. At any rate, there never was a moment's discussion

75 as to whether the atomic bomb should be used or not. To avert a vast, indefinite butchery, to bring the war to an end, to give peace to the world, to lay healing hands upon its tortured peoples by a manifestation of overwhelming power at the cost

80 of a few explosions, seemed, after all our toils and perils, a miracle of deliverance.

GO ON TO THE NEXT PAGE

British consent in principle to the use of the weapon had been given on July 4, before the test had taken place. The final decision now lay in the
85 main with President Truman, who had the weapon; but I never doubted what it would be, nor have I ever doubted since that he was right. The historic fact remains, and must be judged in the aftertime, that the decision whether or not to use the atomic
90 bomb to compel the surrender of Japan was never an issue. There was unanimous, automatic, unquestioned agreement around our table; nor did I ever hear the slightest suggestion that we should do otherwise.
95   A more intricate question was what to tell Stalin. The President and I no longer felt we needed his aid to conquer Japan. . . . [A] continuous movement of Russian troops to the Far East had been in progress over the Siberian Railway since
100 the beginning of May. In our opinion they were not likely to be needed, and Stalin's bargaining power, which he had used with effect . . . was therefore gone. Still, he had been a magnificent ally in the war against Hitler, and we both felt that he must
105 be informed of the great New Fact which now dominated the scene, but not of any particulars. . . . "I think," [the President] said, "I had best just tell him . . . that we have an entirely novel form of bomb, something quite out of the ordinary, which
110 we think will have decisive effects upon the Japanese will to continue the war." I agreed to this procedure.

1. Approximately how much time passed between the first successful test of the atomic bomb and the first use of the bomb on Japan?

   (A) one day   (D) two months
   (B) three days   (E) three months
   (C) three weeks

2. The first paragraph suggests that the test explosion was performed in order to

   (A) persuade Japan to surrender immediately
   (B) convince Churchill of the bomb's power
   (C) test the effects of the bomb on humans
   (D) decide where an explosion would be most effective
   (E) determine how destructive the bomb was

3. Churchill's description of the test explosion suggests that the scientists at the test site reacted to the test results with

   (A) horror   (D) disbelief
   (B) satisfaction   (E) frustration
   (C) disappointment

4. Which did NOT occur prior to the test of the atomic bomb in the desert?

   (A) British and American troops began an invasion of Japan.
   (B) Russian troops began moving toward Japan.
   (C) The Japanese were defeated on Okinawa island.
   (D) Britain gave its approval to using an atomic bomb in the war.
   (E) Truman and Churchill conferred on a plan to defeat Japan.

5. In line 70, "abridgment" most nearly means

   (A) method
   (B) uncertainty
   (C) increase
   (D) reduction
   (E) decision

6. In the passage, Churchill stresses the idea that the main reason to use the atomic bomb was that

   (A) no country would ever again challenge the power of democratic nations
   (B) use of the bomb was consistent with the principles of the United Nations
   (C) although more Japanese would die, far fewer British and American lives would be lost
   (D) failing to do so would give the Russians too much authority in the war effort
   (E) doing so would save the lives of many Allied and Japanese troops

7. Churchill's feelings toward Stalin could be best described as

   (A) indifferent
   (B) sympathetic
   (C) respectful but wary
   (D) cordial and admiring
   (E) frightened and alarmed

8. The passage suggests that, before using the bomb, it was important to Truman to obtain

   (A) Stalin's consent to its use
   (B) Churchill's consent to its use
   (C) the United Nations' consent to its use
   (D) a Russian commitment to fight Japan
   (E) agreement on a postwar plan for Europe

READING TEST

The Struggle for Equality

15 Minutes

DIRECTIONS: After reading the following passage, choose the best
answer to each question and circle the letter of that answer.

SOCIAL SCIENCE: This passage is excerpted from Harvard Sitkoff's work *The Struggle for Black Equality 1954–80* (©1981 by Harvard Sitkoff). The passage focuses on the causes of the growing militancy of some civil rights groups and activists in the mid-1960's.

After the Selma campaign, the leading organizations of the movement had floundered in their search for new programs. Everyone agreed on the need to move beyond the traditional civil-rights
5 agenda. But none developed a viable strategy for solving the complex problems of inadequate housing, dead-end jobs, no jobs, and inferior schooling. A sense of irrelevancy particularly rankled the dedicated activists in CORE and SNCC.
10 They considered themselves the cutting edge of the movement, yet they now stood still. They yearned to lead the struggle to improve the living conditions of poor rural and ghetto blacks, but did not know how. They had paid too high a price in
15 suffering and bloodshed to confess futility, so their impotence festered and turned bitter.

In the midst of this malaise, the young militants abandoned their former beliefs and ideals. Continued school and residential segregation con-
20 vinced the disenchanted blacks that King's goal of an integrated society was an impossible dream. Embittered, they took the growth of the white backlash as proof of the hopeless position of blacks in America. SNCC and CORE began to believe they
25 had to transform the struggle for desegregation into a battle for self-determination. They would have to engage in grass-roots organizing that built the power of black communities and enabled blacks to control their own destinies. Whites could
30 not help in this endeavor. Indeed, the militants concluded that the participation of white liberals had harmed the movement. It had led to the militants' humiliations at the March on Washington and the 1964 Democratic convention. White volunteers had
35 undermined the initiative of Mississippi blacks and reinforced their feelings of inferiority during the Freedom Summer. White liberals had continually

forced the black leaders to compromise and temporize to suit the needs of the Kennedy and
40 Johnson Administrations. Clearly, to the militants, the new liberation struggle required a restricted and subordinate role for whites, if not their total exclusion.

The movement radicals also adopted
45 McKissick's description of nonviolence as "a dying philosophy" that had "outlived its usefulness." They had turned the other cheek too often, with too little to show for it. Traumatized by years of pain and fear, by too many vicious beatings and jailings at
50 the hands of sadistic sheriffs, by too many funerals for close friends killed by white racists, the militants in CORE and SNCC eagerly trumpeted their new inalienable right of self-defense. After the Watts riot, that concept rapidly metamorphized
55 into the doctrine of retaliatory violence. Ultimately, it would blossom into the advocacy of violence as a legitimate tactic wherever feasible.

In charting this new course, the young militants borrowed much from the New Left and even
60 more from Malcolm X. The rhetoric of CORE and SNCC often seemed indistinguishable from that of the Students for a Democratic Society in its condemnation of the Vietnam War, criticism of capitalism, rejection of bourgeois values, and
65 attack on liberalism as the problem rather than the answer. Mostly, SNCC and CORE's new thrust resembled that of Malcolm X. On February 20, 1965, as Malcolm approached the lectern in Harlem's Audubon Ballroom to address a meeting
70 of his Organization for Afro-American Unity, three men affiliated with Elijah Muhammed's Black Muslims had suddenly risen from their seats in the front row and, like a firing squad, felled Malcolm X with their shotgun and
75 revolvers. Several months later, his autobiography appeared. An extraordinary account of his life and exposition of beliefs, *The Autobiography of Malcolm X* immediately swept Black America and profoundly influenced the young in the ghetto
80 and in the movement. In death, Malcolm X

achieved an eminence and a devoted following that he had never had in his lifetime.

Malcolm's separatism articulated the mood of blacks whose hopes had been dashed. "The Negro 85 was really in exile in America," he had repeatedly insisted. "No, I'm not an American. I'm one of the 22 million black people who are the victims of Americanism," he had lashed his critics. "And I see America through the eyes of the victim. I don't see 90 any American dream; I see an American night-mare." Malcolm's black nationalism crystallized the feelings of those whose expectations had been frustrated. Over and over he had emphasized how racism had brainwashed the blacks. "We must 95 revamp our entire thinking and redirect our learn-ing trends so that we can put forth a confident identity and wipe out the false image built up by an oppressive society." Pride in blackness, pride in the Afro-Americans' roots in Africa, and pride in 100 the blacks' capacity to control their own destinies had been his primary teachings.

1. In line 5, the word *viable* most nearly means:
   A. popular.
   B. workable.
   C. destructive.
   D. insignificant.

2. According to the passage, militant leaders found their main sources of inspiration in:
   I. the New Left.
   II. the teachings of Malcolm X.
   III. the teachings of Martin Luther King, Jr.

   F. I and II only
   G. II only
   H. II and III only
   J. I, II, and III

3. At the end of the first paragraph, the author conveys the idea that the activists became bitter because:
   A. despite all of their efforts, they had come to a dead end and felt powerless.
   B. they were tired of making sacrifices and no longer cared about the movement.
   C. they were too exhausted to see that they had actually accomplished a great deal.
   D. they were too close to the situation to view it objectively.

4. The author suggests that Malcolm X was primarily interested in changing the attitudes of:
   F. white people toward themselves.
   G. white people toward African Americans.
   H. African Americans toward themselves.
   J. African Americans toward white people.

5. According to the passage, those leaders and groups who sought to inspire a sense of black pride and a growth in black power had as their ultimate goal:
   A. an end to racial consciousness.
   B. greater respect from white people.
   C. black people's ability to control their own destinies.
   D. a more rapid and complete integration into the dominant, white society.

6. The first paragraph suggests that, immediately after the Selma campaign, the main question faced by civil rights activists was:
   F. Have we achieved enough?
   G. What problems remain?
   H. Who can we count on to lead and inspire us?
   J. How can the remaining problems be solved?

7. The passage suggests that the teachings of Malcolm X emphasized the:
   A. limits of African Americans.
   B. isolation of African Americans.
   C. capabilities of African Americans.
   D. recent gains made by African Americans.

8. This passage suggests that Malcolm X believed that the solution to racism in America would be provided by:
   F. the intellectual elite among African Americans.
   G. African Americans working hand-in-hand with sympathetic white American liberals.
   H. African Americans working hand-in-hand with each other and with oppressed peoples throughout the world.
   J. decisions of the Supreme Court, congressional acts, and orders handed down by the president.

Political Development Around the World

This passage is from a magazine article entitled "The Delicate Birth of a Democracy," which offers a view of political developments around the world. The passage is followed by questions based on its content. Answer the questions on the basis of what is *stated* or *implied* in the passage.

Americans are convinced that democracies make the best foreign-policy partners, and U.S. foreign policy today is primarily concerned with increasing the number of democracies around the
5 world.

Look for the common thread that connects our South Africa policy with our Russia policy with our China policy with our Bosnia policy. The commitment to "enlarging democracy" is the
10 consistent centerpiece of what Washington is trying to do.

This consensus has been taking shape under presidents of both parties, going back to Jimmy Carter's decision to make human rights the key
15 theme of his presidency. Ronald Reagan and GOP foreign-policy intellectuals started out scoffing at Carter's naive, goody-goody approach, but by the end of the Reagan administration, the United States had helped drive Ferdinand E. Marcos out
20 of the Philippines. When European communism collapsed in 1989-1990, the Bush administration made the consolidation of democracy in the former communist states the keystone of its European policy, and the Clinton administration
25 has followed suit.

At the most basic level, this makes sense. Americans believe in democracy and believe that a world of democracies will be more peaceful than a world of dictatorships. Few of America's
30 real quarrels, now or ever, have been with democratic states.

The world, however, is a messy place. . . . Democracy is much harder to build than most Americans like to think. Beyond a handful of
35 countries in Eastern Europe, not many new democracies have taken shape in the last four—or even 14—years.

Instead we find ourselves talking about "emerging" democracies. That is, we see beautiful
40 democratic butterflies clawing their way out of authoritarian cocoons. It is a lovely and comforting metaphor, but countries take longer than butterflies to escape their cocoons. Sometimes much longer.
45 When butterflies escape their cocoons, it's a

one-way trip. But butterflies don't turn back into caterpillars. With countries, it's different. Some are more like groundhogs than butterflies: They emerge for a few minutes, see their shadows and
50 head back to the cave.

Take Africa. At independence, most of Africa started out with democratic regimes. Today, democracy is an endangered species; most African countries are ruled by corrupt, one-party regimes
55 and/or military cliques.

Some people look at this dismal record and claim it proves that third-world countries are too primitive for democracy. Some even draw racist conclusions. That is more than a little unfair.
60 Democracy isn't a mushroom that springs up overnight; it's a tree that must be watered and tended during decades, even centuries, before it can reach its full height.

Look at France. . . . In the 200 years since its
65 Revolution, France has had five republics, four kings and two emperors. Most people now think that France has a stable democracy—but when students and workers riot in Paris, rich Frenchmen, still nervous, ship billions of francs
70 over the Swiss border.

Or look at the United States. How long did it take for democracy to emerge here? Fifty years after the Revolution, many states still denied the vote to everybody who could not meet strict
75 property qualifications. It took 90 years of "democracy" to abolish slavery, over 50 years more to give the vote to women and another some 40 years to guarantee votes to the descendants of former slaves.
80 We need this perspective when we look at the struggles of countries like Mexico, China and Russia. It makes sense for us to have high hopes for the consolidation of democratic values in these countries, but we must not confuse our hopes
85 with our expectations. It is unlikely that any of these countries—or a great many others—will

GO ON TO THE NEXT PAGE

settle down to stable democracy any time soon.

    There are implications here for U.S. foreign policy. It must be based on attainable goals. We
90 should not bark at the moon. While furthering democracy in other countries can and should play a role in U.S. diplomacy, we can't base our global strategy on the illusion that the permanent victory of democracy is just around the corner. Instead we
95 have to be satisfied with small gains, and make foreign policy for a world in which our values are not and will not soon be universal.

    That will require patience, long-term thinking and subtle distinctions.

1. According to the passage, Americans' self-interest is served by encouraging democracies because democracies tend

(A) not to go to war with each other
(B) to result in strong, stable governments
(C) to have economies based on capitalism
(D) to oppose communist governments
(E) to commit few human rights violations

2. In comparing some emerging democracies to groundhogs (lines 47–50), the author is pointing out that these democracies

(A) face more challenges than are present in other countries
(B) emerge only temporarily and are defeated by the problems they face
(C) are sturdier than the fragile democracies in other countries
(D) are viewed by other countries as having meaning for their own futures
(E) are more primitive and less appealing than in other countries

3. The author uses the examples of democracy in France and the United States to stress that

(A) democracy is the most stable form of government
(B) democracy is a product of the nineteenth century
(C) democracies are rooted in the violence of revolution
(D) it may take decades or even centuries for a nation to become truly democratic
(E) authoritarian nations can become democratic only by forming partnerships with other democratic nations

4. The word "consensus" (line 12) most nearly means

(A) main idea
(B) compromise
(C) achievement
(D) misconception
(E) general agreement

5. Which statement best summarizes the argument the author makes in this passage?

(A) Democracies can take a long time to develop and face many challenges along the way.
(B) Democracies are fragile political structures that may not withstand serious challenges.
(C) Nature is the major determining factor in whether political structures can change.
(D) People who try to describe governments in simplistic terms are doomed to fail.
(E) All American foreign policy has essentially the same goal, regardless of who is in power.

6. The author contrasts democracies with butterflies and mushrooms in order to note that democracies

(A) are less fragile
(B) are created by humans
(C) take much longer to develop
(D) occur with less frequency
(E) cannot be easily defeated

7. In the paragraph beginning "Or look . . ." (line 71), the author suggests that the United States

(A) has yet to qualify as a democracy
(B) has made consistent efforts to strengthen its own democracy
(C) has faced many challenges to its status as a democracy
(D) must change with the times to remain a true democracy
(E) was not a true democracy until equality in voting rights was achieved

Early River Valley Civilizations

The passage below is followed by questions based on its content. Answer the questions on the basis of what is *stated* or *implied* in the passage and in any introductory material that may be provided.

This passage is from a book exploring some of the great mysteries of world history. It describes a civilization that existed from about 2500 B.C. to about 1500 B.C. along the Indus River in present day Pakistan.

Harappa and Mohenjo-Daro, which both cover hundreds of acres, are the two most important known urban centers of the Indus civilization. In addition there are about another 100 known sites
5 which either belonged to the same culture or ere strongly influenced by it. Few of these cover more than 24 acres. Most are situated in Pakistan though some have been found in India. . . .

The layout of Indus settlements is regular,
10 with streets crossing one another at right angles. The plan of the buildings and the materials are severely functional with little ornamentation. The larger cities and towns each seem to have been divided into districts, each principally housing
15 workers of a particular trade.

This leads to the conclusion that the cities were conceived almost in their entirety before they were built. There was no room for fussy additions or whims, and scrupulous care was
20 taken over matters of hygiene and utility. In short, the Indus cities are the first manifestation of town planning. . . .

It is thought that Mohenjo-Daro at its peak must have housed some 40,000 inhabitants, a
25 substantial number for an era and a place in which the principal sources of wealth were agricultural land and domestic animals. But the city itself was a commercial metropolis serving an extensive territory.

30 More astonishing than its extent is the grid-plan: a fabric of streets about ten yards wide running from north to south and from east to west formed rectangular blocks of roughly equal size, about 400 x 300 yards. From this it is an easy
35 step, if not strictly correct in a scientific sense, to imagine the inhabitants of Mohenjo-Daro measuring distances by blocks in the modern American manner. . . .

Impressive as its size and regularity may be,
40 Mohenjo-Daro possessed another, equally admirable attribute: It had a complex sanitary and sewage system. For the people of Mohenjo-Daro developed both public and private hygiene to a remarkable degree, one unparalleled in pre-classical
45 times and still unmatched in many parts of the world today. Most private dwellings, for example, both large and small, were equipped with a special kind of trash chute that was built into one of the outside walls and passed through to the street.
50 These chutes allowed householders to slide debris into small individual gutters outside, and these gutters in turn were connected to a covered central sewer system.

At intervals along the central system there
55 were sumps, or drainage pits, designed to collect the heaviest waste so that it would not obstruct the main passageways. In addition, wells were liberally placed throughout the city, some directly accessible from the streets and therefore public,
60 some constructed as part of individual houses and thus reserved for private use.

What was life like in Mohenjo-Daro and the other cities? It was undoubtedly austere, tending towards trade and labor rather than festivals the
65 arts, and the sweet life. All the houses were alike in their basic plan. The only difference between the home of the rich merchant and that of the poor craftsman was in their size and in a few technical refinements. The overall impression is
70 one of perfect coherence a coherence amounting to uniformity. The miles of uninterrupted brickwork would have been featureless, and the absence of any kind of meeting place-apart from the streets and what might have been an eating
75 hall in Mohenjo Daro-adds to the impression of monotony. . . .

In many ways the cities of the Indus remain mysterious, and the supply of certainties about the Harappan culture is almost as thin as the supply
80 of theories is inexhaustible. There are several theories as to how the civilization ended, and it is likely that there were several contributory causes. It has been suggested that a spectacular rise in the

GO ON TO THE NEXT PAGE ➡

waters of the Indus (such as still occurs today)
85 finally overcame the energy of the people who had
previously been determined to keep the river under
control. On the other hand, it has been suggested
than an Aryan invasion, occurring around 1500 B.C.,
was responsible for the decline. Neither of these
90 two arguments has completely convinced
archaeologists working on the Harappan culture.
It seems that both explanations are too simple to
account for the eclipse of such a well-organized
society; moreover, there is evidence of a general
95 decline over a period of 500 years before the arrival
of the Aryans. Some have suggested that the
abandonment of the two major cities was directly
related to an in internal breakdown of the political
and economic institutions that long distinguished
100 the society.

1. According to the author, both Harappa and
Mohenjo-Daro were

   (A) the only cities in the Indus civilization
   (B) capital cities
   (C) impressive urban centers
   (D) cities in decline economically and politically
   (E) primarily large agricultural towns

2. In line 63 the author uses the word "austere" to note
that life in Mohenjo-Daro was

   (A) coherent
   (B) mysterious
   (C) highly advanced
   (D) well-organized
   (E) very plain

3. What evidence does the author cite to support the
conclusion that the cities of the Indus were
planned?

   (A) Settlements were located along rivers for
        purposes of trade.
   (B) All houses were similar in layout.
   (C) Few cities covered more than 24 acres.
   (D) Temples were accessible from all parts of the
        city.
   (E) Wells were located throughout the city.

4. This passage suggests that Mohenjo-Daro was

   (A) home to many different religions
   (B) a cultural center
   (C) a center of learning and higher education
   (D) a center of commerce and trade
   (E) a military city-state

5. According to the author, one of the most admirable
characteristics of Harappan society was its

   (A) sanitation system
   (B) traditions and customs
   (C) functional building materials
   (D) domesticated animals
   (E) large eating halls

6. In the Indus settlements, the streets were laid out to
form

   (A) city centers and outlying areas
   (B) drainage pits and gutters
   (C) agricultural and residential areas
   (D) rectangular blocks of approximately the same
        size
   (E) public meeting areas

7. The passage suggests that people living in
Mohenjo-Daro may have measured distances by
using

   (A) Arabic numerals
   (B) acres
   (C) yards and miles
   (D) a complex scientific system
   (E) American-type city blocks

8. The statement in lines 78–80 that "the supply of
certainties about the Harappan culture is almost as
thin as the supply of theories is inexhaustible"
means that

   (A) most information about Harappan culture is
        guesswork
   (B) there are more theories about Harappan culture
        than there are facts
   (C) many theories about this early culture are not
        logical
   (D) there are too many sites for archaeologists to
        study
   (E) the study of ancient cultures constantly reveals
        new information

9. The author thinks it is most probable that the Indus
civilization collapsed because of

   (A) floods
   (B) invasion
   (C) many contributing factors
   (D) loss of trade
   (E) political turmoil

READING TEST

The Roman Empire

15 Minutes

DIRECTIONS: This test has one passage followed by ten multiple-choice questions. After reading the passage, choose the best answer to each question and circle the letter of that answer. Refer to the passage as often as you wish while answering the questions.

By the middle of the first century B.C. Rome was a cesspool of political intrigue and civic turmoil. The only good news, it seemed, came from distant battlefields and people waited
5 eagerly for each new from afar. Caesar, who could write as skillful he fought, turned the composition of military patches into an art form. The triumph of the was his immortal message back to' Rome after trouncing the Parthinians at Zela in 47 B.C.:
10 *Veni, vidi, vici*-I came, I.saw, I conquered.". . .

When Caesar led his army across the Rubicon River in 49 B.C., defying the orders of the senate, it seemed clear that he would seize absolute power. The conspirators who slew him on the ides of
15 March, 44 B.C., probably believed they were acting to save Roman democracy.

In fact, they merely launched another long civil war. In the end Julius Caesar's onetime sidekick Mark Antony ... was defeated at the battle
20 of Actium in 31 B.C. The victor, Octavian, returned to Rome, assumed the august name "Augustus," and eventually established one-man rule—with the once proud senate serving as his rubber stamp. The imperial court Caesar Augustus created would
25 continue for another four centuries at Rome and ten more after the move to Constantinople.

Many ancient nations—and many modern ones—experienced the same sort of turbulent transition from democracy to dictatorship, or vice
30 versa. But Rome's vast foreign empire remained intact—indeed thrived—throughout all the upheaval at home. This is where Rome broke the mold of Western history.

Far to the east the Chinese created a huge land
35 empire in the centuries before Christ. But the Western world, since the dawn of recorded history, had been a world of city-states—of smaller, independent political entities. They regularly sacked and pillaged one another but did
40 not seek a wide hegemony. There were alliances but no great empires until Alexander the Great

bestrode western Asia in the fourth century B.C. Alexander's empire was a distinguished personal achievement, but it could not survive its founder.
45 The Romans, in contrast, proved to be master empire builders.

Historians have been debating since ancient times just how Rome came to rule the Western world. In the second century B.C. the Greek author
50 Pylorus devoted 40 volumes to the question and concluded that Rome was driven by a concept of manifest destiny, a compulsion to dominate. The Romans themselves, such as the statesman-philosopher Cicero, generally maintained that
55 theirs was an accidental empire, acquired in the process of defending against invaders.

The Roman Empire began, at least, in this haphazard way. Centuries of skirmishes against rival states gradually expanded Roman territory,
60 and by the third century B.C. most of Italy was under Roman dominion-a development that probably surprised the Romans as much as the more established city-states of the Mediterranean world.

65 "If you're standing in the middle of the fourth century wondering who's going to conquer the world, you're definitely not going to bet on Rome," Professor Wallace-Hadrill, the British historian, told me. "The great powers were the famous city
70 states—Alexandria, Athens, Syracuse, Carthage. They had the great navies, which Rome didn't have. But the Romans had their army, and they had this is doggedness about them. They kept fight these border wars, and they kept winning.
75 and when they had conquered the world, they turned out to be cleverer than anybody else at organization and maintaining an empire."

Driven by political pressure and economic need—for rain, for slaves, for metals, for fabric,
80 etc.—Roman expansion shifted into high gear after 260 B.C. One by one the great states of the Mediterranean fell before the steady onslaught of

the Roman legions, with their catapults and flame
thrower and highly disciplined foot soldiers
85 marching relentlessly forward in centuries (blocks
of shielded men).

In just 200 years Rome extended its sway from
Syria to Spain, from southern France to the
Sahara. Long before Augustus became first Roman
90 emperor, the empire was largely in place. A few
provinces would be added later at the margins—
Britannia, Dacia (western Romania), Armenia. But
the real task facing Augustus and his successors
was not gaining the empire but governing it.

95 And government, as it happened, turned out
to be the supreme Roman an talent. Although
Romans produced deathless less poetry and prose,
sublime paintings, and mosaics so perfect they take
your breath away, Rome always felt a collective
100 inferiority complex toward Greece in the realms of
art, literature, and science. But government—that
was different. This was an art form Romans could
master.

from T. R. Reid, "The Power and the Glory of the Roman
Empire," *National Geographic* (July 1997), 2-41.

1. The first Roman Emperor was:

   A. Alexander the Great.   **C.** Caesar Augustus.
   B. Julius Caesar.   **D.** Mark Antony.

2. According to the author, Caesar's message *"Veni
vidi, vici"* in line 10 reveals Caesar's:

   F. defiance of the Roman senate.
   G. skill as a military commander.
   H. talent for writing great military dispatches.
   J. ability to govern.

3. This passage focuses primarily on which of the
following?

   A. Cultural achievements of the Roman Empire
   B. Rome's military and political achievements
   C. Julius Caesar and Caesar Augustus
   D. The power of the city-states

4. As it is used in line 21, the word "august" means:

   F. dictatorial.   **H.** immortal
   G. turbulent.   **J.** majestic.

5. According to the passage, which of the following
factors probably motivated Romans to build a great
empire?

   I. belief in manifest destiny
   II. Economic need
   III. Political pressures at home
   A. I and II only   **C.** II and III only
   B. II only   **D.** I, II, and III

6. The author conveys the idea that the major
difference between the Roman Empire and earlier
empires was that the Roman Empire was:

   F. able to survive during times of civic turmoil at
home.
   G. the personal achievement of one military leader.
   H. able to change from a dictatorship to a
democracy.
   J. not based on alliances.

7. According to the author, the greatest achievement of
the Romans was:

   A. expanding their empire.
   B. organizing and governing their empire.
   C. maintaining a disciplined army.
   D. conquering the world.

8. Is the following statement (lines 99–101) treated in
the passage as an established fact?

   . . . Rome always felt a collective inferiority
complex toward Greece in the realms of art,
literature, and science.

   F. No, because it is a personal judgment and
cannot be verified.
   G. No, because historians are still debating this
point.
   H. Yes, because Greek culture was more advanced
than was Roman culture.
   J. Yes, because this passage comes from a reliable
source.

9. The passage suggests that the assassins of Julius
Caesar:

   A. ushered in a period of civil upheaval.
   B. saved Roman democracy.
   C. defended the empire against foreign invasion.
   D. united the Mediterranean city-states.

10. The observation by Cicero that the Roman empire
was an "accidental empire" (line 55) means that the
empire was created as a result of:

   F. political intrigue and internal upheaval.
   G. romantic alliances such as that of Antony and
Cleopatra.
   H. defensive military victories.
   J. sacking and pillaging neighboring city-states.

West African Empire

This passage is from a book about three great West African empires: Ghana, Mali, and Songhai. It deals with Mansa Musa I, who was king of Mali during the 1300s. The passage is followed by questions based on its content. Answer the questions on the basis of what is *stated* or *implied* in the passage.

Probably the greatest of all the Keita kings of Mali was Mansa Kankan Musa I. Musa's mother's name was Kongo, and Musa is Arabic for Moses, so sometimes he was called Kongo Musa, or
5 Moses, Son of Kongo. During his reign, which began in 1307 and lasted twenty-five years, he doubled the land area of Mali. Known as the khan of Africa, Musa governed an empire as large as all of Europe, second in size only to the territory at
10 the time ruled by Genghis Khan in Asia.

Mali was divided into provinces, just as Ghana had been before it. Musa appointed governors called *ferbas* to manage the day-to-day operations of these regions. Each important town had
15 inspectors called *mochrifs,* and there were royal tax collectors stationed at every marketplace.

Trade tripled in Mali during Mansa Musa's reign. The whole Sudan was crisscrossed by trade routes, bringing caravans from the four corners of
20 the known world. Camel trains emerged out of the desert, bringing goods, news, and visitors to Mali's markets. . . .

One of the religious obligations a Muslim is required to fulfill is a *hajj,* a pilgrimage to Mecca
25 and Medina, the holy cities of Islam. Mansa Musa was a devout Muslim, so he made plans for his hajj in 1324.

Although Arabia had been trading with Africans below the Sahara for centuries, this trip
30 gave them their first extended view of a West African ruler, and it left a lasting impression. The details of the famous hajj were recorded by al-Umari (1301-1349), a chronicler from Cairo. In his *Masalik al-Ahsad,* he described Musa's
35 caravan as "a lavish display of power, wealth, and unprecedented by its size and pageantry." Al-Umari, however, was in Syria at the time of the hajj, so he collected his information from Egyptian officials, religious leaders, ordinary
40 citizens, and merchants who had talked with Mansa Musa.

Months before Mansa Musa's departure from Mali, officials and servants began preparing for the long trip. Five hundred slaves, each carrying a
45 six-pound staff of gold, arrived in Cairo, Egypt, in July of 1324. Next came Musa and his entourage,

followed by a caravan of one hundred camels, each carrying three hundred pounds of gold. A hundred more camels carried food, clothing, and
50 other supplies. All together sixty thousand people accompanied the mansa to Mecca.

Mansa Musa reached Cairo after eight months of travel. His Arab guide suggested that he visit the local ruler or sultan. Musa rejected the idea,
55 saying he wasn't interested in making a social call. The guide convinced him that his actions might be taken as an insult by an important Muslim brother. So Musa agreed to make the visit.

It was customary that a visitor kneel and kiss
60 the ground before the Sultan. Mansa Musa flatly refused. He was richer and controlled more territory than the sultan of Egypt, so why, he asked, should he kowtow before a lesser king? Once again, the guide explained the custom to
65 Musa. "Very well," Musa agreed, choosing diplomacy. "I will prostrate myself before Allah, who created me and brought me into the world." Having done this, the sultan compromised too. He welcomed Musa to come sit beside him, a sign
70 that they were equals.

Musa continu\ed to Arabia, where he completed his hajj. Merchants and travelers had teased Middle Easterners with stories about the gold-rich empires below the Sahara. When news
75 spread that the king of Mali was in the city, people lined the streets to see him.

Everywhere Mansa Musa went he graciously paid for every service in gold and gave lavish gifts to his hosts. Merchants scrambled to get his
80 attention, for it was not uncommon for Musa to buy up everything that was presented to him. Beggars lined the streets as he passed, hoping to receive a gold nugget.

By the time Mansa Musa left the Middle East,
85 he had put so much gold into circulation, its value fell sharply. A reporter in the service of the Egyptian sultan reported that the Cairo gold market had been so saturated that it still had not

GO ON TO THE NEXT PAGE

fully recovered twelve years after Mansa Musa's
90 fabulous hajj.

1. According to the author, Mansa Musa ruled over

   (A) the largest empire in the world
   (B) the largest empire in Europe
   (C) an empire as large as Asia
   (D) an empire second in size to that of Genghis
       Khan
   (E) the only Muslim empire in Africa

2. In this passage, the author suggests that al-Umari's
   account of Mansa Musa's hajj may not be entirely
   accurate because al-Umari

   (A) had received gold nuggets from Mansa Musa
   (B) was not a devout Muslim
   (C) relied on information from people who had
       spoken with Mansa Musa
   (D) wrote the account months before Mansa Musa
       arrived in Mecca
   (E) worked for the Egyptian sultan

3. In line 46, "entourage" refers to

   (A) a camel caravan
   (B) gold coins
   (C) food, clothing, and supplies
   (D) the people accompanying Musa
   (E) lavish gifts

4. Approximately how much time elapsed between
   Mansa Musa's departure from Mali and his arrival
   in Cairo?

   (A) eight weeks
   (B) six months
   (C) eight months
   (D) one year
   (E) twenty-five years

5. According to the passage, what was the primary
   reason why Mansa Musa refused to kneel before
   the Egyptian sultan?

   (A) Mansa Musa was richer and more powerful than
       the sultan.
   (B) Mansa Musa considered himself an equal to the
       sultan.
   (C) Mansa Musa did not understand the Egyptian
       custom.
   (D) The sultan had insulted Mansa Musa.
   (E) Mansa Musa was anxious to continue on to
       Arabia.

6. Why were the people in Arabia so eager to see
   Mansa Musa?

   (A) They had never seen a camel caravan before.
   (B) They wanted to pray with this respected Muslim
       leader.
   (C) They had read about his achievements in
       al-Umari's chronicles.
   (D) They hoped to receive gifts and gold from him.
   (E) They wanted to learn more about the holy cities
       of Islam.

7. According to this passage, which of the following
   does NOT describe Mansa Musa?

   (A) religious
   (B) diplomatic
   (C) charitable
   (D) powerful
   (E) intolerant

8. A a result of Mansa Musa's hajj to the Middle East,

   (A) Arabia became wealthier than Mali
   (B) the value of gold declined
   (C) the demand for gold declined
   (D) new trade routes developed south of the Sahara
   (E) the number of pilgrimages increased

The Age of Enlightenment

The passage below is followed by questions based on its content. Answer the questions on the basis of what is *stated* or *implied* in the passage and in any introductory material that may be provided.

This passage is from a book describing different aspects of the Age of Enlightenment in Europe. The Enlightenment was an age of criticism and questioning, of asking whether society was organized in a sensible way. It measured human institutions against the standard of reason.

In 1784, at the height of the Age of Enlightenment, the German philosopher Immanuel Kant wrote an article for a popular audience explaining the meaning of the word that gave the
5 age its name. "Enlightenment," Kant began, "is man's emergence from his nonage." This nonage, or immaturity, he continued, was caused not by "lack of intelligence, but lack of determination and courage to use that intelligence without another's
10 guidance. *Sapere aude*! Dare to know! Have the courage to use your own intelligence!"

Kant's words summed up the most cherished convictions and ambitious designs of radical 18th Century scholars and intellectuals. His words
15 implied that man was mature enough to find his own way without paternal authority; they urged man to understand his own nature and the natural world by the methods of science. In short, they were a declaration of freedom. Kant and his
20 fellow thinkers wanted men to shake off the hand of authority in politics and religion, and think for themselves.

Kant was called a *philosophe*, a French word that did not apply to Frenchmen alone. From
25 Scotland to Naples an impressive clan of radical intellectuals had become passionate and outspoken partisans of the new philosophy of John Locke and the new science of Isaac Newton. They were hostile to organized Christianity,
30 and said so; they openly deplored cruel legal procedures and arbitrary government; they believed in freedom of speech and the press, and in personal liberty. They were erudite, but they were not above popularizing their views. Kant's
35 article had been preceded by a vigorous campaign conducted by the *philosophes* in country after country, designed to expose the evils of religion and extol the virtues of their own enlightened philosophy.

40 And yet, while the *philosophes* were a clan, they were not a coherent movement. Although they knew one another and corresponded, they did not always think alike. The only thing they had in common was a critical attitude toward any
45 sort of orthodoxy, and especially toward orthodox religion. They did not believe in miracles, and, if they believed in God at all, thought of Him as the mechanic of the universe—a sort of cosmic watchmaker; He had built a superb machine,
50 given it laws to run by and then withdrawn. From such a view it followed that the only reliable road to knowledge of God's plans was through science, not religion, through observation and experiment, not dogma and revelation.

55 Fortunately for the *philosophes'* purpose, their ideas were launched in a cultural atmosphere that was generally favorable to them. Thousands of educated men and women who were good Christians and thoroughly loyal to existing
60 political institutions—men and women, in fact, who had nothing but dislike, and even contempt, for the *philosophes*—nevertheless shared at least some of their attitudes. They were humanitarians, or tepid about religious observances, or critical of
65 government policies. The *philosophes* had many allies who did not know they were allies, people whose cast of mind was compatible with the ultimate goals of the Enlightenment.

Clearly, an age that takes its name from
70 an intellectual atmosphere cannot be fixed within rigid chronological limits. In one sense the Enlightenment began as far back as the Renaissance, with men's renewed interest in Greek and Latin texts, their critical approach to medieval
75 Christian philosophy and their general sense of curiosity about this world as opposed to the next. Even the Protestant Reformation, despite its call for a return to the beliefs of early Christianity, helped to prepare the way for the Enlightenment
80 by disrupting the unity of Western Christendom and weakening the authority of the Church.

GO ON TO THE NEXT PAGE

During the 17th Century philosophers tried to weld the consequences of these intellectual developments into a new kind of philosophy,
85 distinct from the Christian worldview of medieval theologians. It was this century, too, that elaborated the new science—and without science and reason the Enlightenment would have been unthinkable. In fact, if a single point in time must be assigned
90 as the start of the Enlightenment, no date could be more logical and fitting than the year of Newton's publication of his widely admired—but intellectually demanding—masterpiece, the *PhilosoPhiae naturalis principia mathematica*
95 *(Mathematical Principles of Natural Philosophy).* That year was 1687.

1. According to the author, the Age of Enlightenment was based on

   (A) science and reason
   (B) hostility to cruel legal procedures
   (C) an accepted world-view
   (D) opposition to existing political institutions
   (E) the writings of Immanuel Kant

2. One reason that the new ideas of the Enlightenment were able to take hold was that

   (A) a unified movement already existed
   (B) the authority of the Church had weakened
   (C) people identified with the *philosophes'* belief in miracles
   (D) many people already agreed with one or more aspects of Enlightenment thinking
   (E) most people were erudite and mature

3. In this passage, the author characterizes 18th Century intellectuals primarily as

   (A) upper class
   (B) lacking in determination
   (C) paternal
   (D) cosmic watchmakers
   (E) outspoken in their beliefs

4. The passage suggests that the ideas of Isaac Newton and John Locke were

   (A) unpopular with the *philosophes*
   (B) consistent with the ideas of the Enlightenment
   (C) renounced by humanitarians
   (D) promoted by the Church
   (E) rooted in the ideas of the Renaissance

5. According to the author, Enlightenment thinkers wanted people to

   (A) renew their interest in Greek and Latin
   (B) accept authority in government
   (C) follow dogma and revelation
   (D) think for themselves
   (E) become scientists

6. In line 31, "arbitrary" most nearly means

   (A) unreasonable
   (B) strong
   (C) hostile
   (D) constitutional
   (E) disruptive

7. Enlightenment thinkers believed that knowledge was the result of

   (A) understanding mathematical principles
   (B) observing and experimenting
   (C) reading and discussing the classics
   (D) campaigning for personal freedoms
   (E) developing a sense of curiosity about the next world

8. The passage suggests that the Enlightenment actually began with the

   (A) Renaissance
   (B) popularization of the ideas of the *philosophes*
   (C) publication of Newton's *Mathematical Principles of Natural Philosophy*
   (D) publication of John Locke's new philosophy
   (E) emergence of man from his "nonage"

READING TEST

Industrial Revolution: Child Labor

15 Minutes

DIRECTIONS: This test has one passage followed by ten multiple choice questions. After reading the passage, choose the best answer to each question and circle the letter of that answer. Refer to the passage as often as you wish while answering the questions.

Work in the coal breakers is exceedingly hard and dangerous. Crouched over the chutes, the boys sit hour after hour, picking out the pieces of slate and other refuse from the coal as it rushes past to

5 the washers. From the cramped position they have to assume, most of them become more or less deformed and bent-backed like old men. When a boy has been working for some time and begins to get round-shouldered, his fellows say that "He's got

10 his boy to carry round whenever he goes."

The coal is hard, and accidents to the hands, such as cut, broken, or crushed fingers, are common among the boys. Sometimes there is a worse accident: a terrified shriek is heard, and a

15 boy is mangled and torn in the machinery, or disappears in the chute to be picked out later smothered and dead. Clouds of dust fill the breakers and are inhaled by the boys, laying the foundations for asthma and miners' consumption.

20 I once stood in a breaker for half an hour and tried to do the work a twelve-year-old boy was doing day after day, for ten hours at a stretch, for sixty cents a day. The gloom of the breaker appalled me. Outside the sun shone brightly, the

25 air was pellucid, and the birds sang in chorus with the trees and the rivers. Within the breaker there was blackness, clouds of deadly dust enfolded everything, the harsh, grinding roar of the machinery and the ceaseless rushing of coal

30 through the chutes filled the ears. I tried to pick out the pieces of slate from the hurrying stream of coal, often missing them; my hands were bruised and cut in a few minutes; I was covered from head to foot with coal dust, and for many

35 hours afterwards I was expectorating some of the small particles of anthracite I had swallowed.

I could not do that work and live, but there were boys of ten and twelve years of age doing it for fifty and sixty cents a day. Some of them had

40 never been inside of a school; few of them could read a child's primer. True, some of them attended the night schools, but after working ten hours in the breaker the educational results from attending school were practically nil. . . .

45 As I stood in that breaker I thought of the reply of the small boy to Robert Owen. Visiting an English coal mine one day, Owen asked a twelve-year-old lad if he knew God. The boy stared vacantly at his questioner: "God?" he said,

50 "God? No I don't. He must work in some other mine." It was hard to realize amid the danger and the din and blackness of that Pennsylvania breaker that such a thing as belief in a great All-good God existed.

55 From the breakers the boys graduate to the mine depths, where they become door tenders, switch boys, or mule drivers. Here, far below the surface, work is still more dangerous. At fourteen or fifteen the boys assume the same risks as the

60 men, and are surrounded by the same perils. Nor it is in Pennsylvania only that these conditions exist. In the bituminous mines of West Virginia, boys of nine or ten are frequently employed. I met one little fellow ten years old in Mt. Carbon,

65 West Virginia, last year, who was employed as a "trap boy." Think of what it means to be a trap boy at ten years of age. It means to sit alone in a dark mine passage hour after hour, with no human soul near; to see no living creature except

70 the mules as they pass with their loads, or a rat or two seeking to share one's meal; to stand in water or mud that covers the ankles, chilled to the marrow by the cold draughts that rush in when you open the trap door for the mules to pass

75 through; to work for fourteen hours—waiting— opening and shutting a door—then waiting again-for sixty cents; to reach the surface when all is wrapped in the mantle of night, and to fall to the earth exhausted and have to be carried away

80 to the nearest "shack" to be revived before it is possible to walk to the farther shack called "home."

Boys twelve years of age may be *legally* employed in the mines of West Virginia, by day or
85 by night, and for as many hours as the employers care to make them toil or their bodies will stand the strain. Where the disregard of child life is such that this may be done openly and with legal sanction, it is easy to believe what miners have
90 again and again told me-that there are hundreds of little boys of nine and ten years of age employed in the coal mines of this state.

from John Spargo, *The Bitter Cry of the Children* (New York: Macmillan, 1906), 163-165.

1. The main purpose of this passage is to:
   A. convince mine owners in Pennsylvania and West Virginia to close the mines.
   B. get higher wages for the children.
   C. expose hazardous working conditions for children in the coal mines.
   D. encourage more children to attend school.

2. The author uses the quotation in lines 9 and 10 to illustrate the fact that:
   F. young boys recognized the consequences of the conditions under which they worked.
   G. despite dangerous working conditions, young miners kept their senses of humor.
   H. men often carried the boys into the mines on their backs.
   J. boys were frequently killed by the machinery.

3. According to the passage, when boys reached the ages of 14 or 15, they worked:
   A. in the coal breakers separating the coal.
   B. as trap boys.
   C. in the coal chutes with the machinery.
   D. alongside the men below the surface.

4. The passage suggests that in the early 1900s:
   F. young children were not allowed to join labor unions.
   G. young girls could work in textile factories, but not in coal mines.
   H. boys competed with each other to obtain work in the coal mines.
   J. state legislatures had not passed child labor laws.

5. According to the passage, all of the following as: conditions applied to the work of a trap boy EXCEPT:
   A. feeling lonely and cold.
   B. standing ankle-deep in water.
   C. being mangled by machinery.
   D. working long hours in darkness.

6. In lines 45–54, the conversation between Robert Owen and the child miner is used to illustrate the author's observation that the child:
   F. had not been taught Christian religion.
   G. could not read the Bible.
   H. was rude because he had no education.
   J. could not hear the question over the din of the machinery.

7. The author was especially understanding of the plight of the children working in the mines because:
   A. his own family could not live on sixty cents a day.
   B. he had spent part of a day picking out pieces of slate from coal.
   C. he had a terrible accident in an English coal mine.
   D. he suffered miner's consumption.

8. In line 44, the word "nil" is used to describe the:
   F. number of children attending night school.
   G. ability of children to learn after working all day.
   H. number of children who could read a primer.
   J. quality of education in Pennsylvania and West Virginia.

9. According to the passage, which of the following conditions contributed to the bleak existence of child miners?
   I. Poor housing
   II. Exhausting work
   III. Lack of fellowship
   IV. Pellucid air in the mines

   A. I and II only
   B. I and III only
   C. II and III only
   D. I, II, and III only

10. In this passage, the author views mine owners
    F. appalled by the living conditions of mining families.
    G. supportive of higher wages.
    H. unconcerned about child welfare.
    J. unaware of accidents in the coal breakers.

ACT/SAT 1 Answer Key

Page 74: The Spanish, Amerindians, and Smallpox (SAT)

1. A
2. B
3. E
4. A
5. C
6. B
7. A
8. B
9. D

Page 76: Creating a Nation (ACT)

1. B
2. H
3. A
4. H
5. D
6. G
7. B
8. J
9. A
10. J
11. B
12. H

Page 78: Plantation Slavery (SAT)

1. A
2. C
3. C
4. E
5. D
6. A
7. A

Page 80: Difference Between American and European Farmers (ACT)

1. D
2. G
3. C
4. J
5. A
6. H
7. C
8. J

Page 82: Wilson, Neutrality, and Intervention (SAT)

1. E
2. B
3. C
4. A
5. D
6. B
7. C

Page 84: Causes and Effects of the Great Depression (ACT)

1. C
2. G
3. C
4. H
5. D
6. G
7. D
8. G
9. A

Page 86: The Atomic Bomb (SAT)

1. C
2. E
3. B
4. A
5. D
6. C
7. C
8. B

Page 88: The Struggle for Equality (ACT)

1. B
2. F
3. A
4. H
5. C
6. J
7. C
8. H

Page 90: Political Development Around the World (SAT)

1. A
2. E
3. D
4. E
5. A
6. C
7. E

Page 92: Early River Valley Civilization (SAT)

1. C
2. E
3. B
4. D
5. A
6. D
7. E
8. B
9. C

Page 94: The Roman Empire (ACT)

1. C
2. H
3. B
4. J
5. D
6. F
7. B
8. F
9. A
10. H

Page 96: West African Empires (SAT)

1. D
2. C
3. D
4. C
5. A
6. D
7. E
8. B

Page 98: The Age Of Enlightenment (SAT)

1. A
2. D
3. E
4. B
5. D
6. A
7. B
8. C

Page 100: Industrial Revolution: Child Labor (ACT)

1. C
2. D
3. E
4. B
5. D
6. A
7. B
8. C
9. D
10. H